Call

to

Commitment

Call

to

Commitment

The Story of
the Church of the Saviour,
Washington, D.C.

by Elizabeth O'Connor

HARPER & ROW, PUBLISHERS

New York, Evanston, and London

To
Mary Cosby
whose life is music in our midst

CONTENTS

FOREWORD

by Elton Trueblood

If an ounce of demonstration is worth a ton of speculation, the story which Elizabeth O'Connor tells is precious, indeed. The Church of the Saviour is the most encouraging Christian fellowship known to me. It is encouraging because it takes seriously the notion that the Church is meant to be a redemptive fellowship rather than a religious equivalent of secular promotion. It started in a combination of anguish and faith, and the founding mood has been miraculously maintained.

The experience of the Church of the Saviour is shocking to many sincere Christians. They are shocked, in the first place, because it is still small in numbers. To remain small when growth is possible is mystifying and faintly un-American. The very conception of making membership genuine rather than nominal, and therefore difficult, is bitterly resented by some, who rightly see this conception as an implicit criticism of their own superficial standards of membership.

When so many Christians have an "edifice complex," it is shocking for a now famous congregation to have no proper church building. The modest structure at 2025 Massachusetts Avenue is not even called a "church." It is simply the "Headquarters" of the Church of the Saviour. In it are library, guest rooms, kitchen, office, etc., but no ecclesiastical atmosphere whatever. The "church" is not confined to a spot on Massachusetts Avenue, but is in the

homes and offices and coffee shop and arts and crafts center and retreat farm. The church is where the members are carrying on their
ministry. They don't need a pipe organ. All who think Christianity
is centered in shrines are almost bound to resent this emphasis, particularly when it is successful.

The feature of the Church of the Saviour which surprises people most is the practice of encouraging strong members either to
work primarily outside the fellowship in mission groups to the unchurched or even to leave and thus be free to join some other fellowship which needs them. The philosophy of this procedure is
clear, even though it goes directly against the grain of ordinary
practice. The usual procedure is to hold firmly to those who have
developed strength, whether spiritual or financial, but this is not
done in the fellowship which Elizabeth O'Connor describes. It is
not done because the clear teaching of Christ is against it. The grain
of wheat does not bear fruit unless it dies. The church which ag-
grandizes itself may seem successful in the eyes of the world, but it
is not thereby loyal to Christ's disturbing dream.

One of the ideas of the author of this book which is, so far as I
know, original is the idea that people can be called to leave a fellowship just as they are called to enter it, and that they should not
leave unless they are thus called. This means that a committed
member will not leave because of wanderlust, or even because of
better opportunities for employment in another city, but only because the opportunity to serve Christ's cause seems greater. The
dedicated Christian will not make this momentous decision alone,
but will seek the prayerful judgment of the group before he acts.
"As there was once a reception service," says our author, "there
would now be a departure service—the farewell of a community
to a brother who is called of God to do a work of God in another
place."

It is highly encouraging to know that the story here told has not
become a denominational story. Many expected that it would. But
Gordon Cosby and his associates have seen the danger and have
been able to avoid it. They do not want to produce another denomination, but to make a demonstration which may have an en-

during effect upon the denominations. They want to create, under God, a fellowship so contagious, that the contagion spreads and spreads within existing organizations, rather than as something in competition with them. Gordon Cosby has aimed for bigness, not in his own organization, but in Christendom as a whole. The only way in which this could have been done was, he saw, a way that is frankly local. Bishop Emrich, of the Episcopal Diocese of Michigan, has put the matter with memorable succinctness: "To make a thing real, make it local," he says. The Church of the Saviour has paid this price of reality.

Many, and especially pastors, are openly envious of the opportunity which Gordon Cosby and his associates have enjoyed. These people say it is easier to make a bold and unequivocal witness in a new church than it would be to do so in an old established church. In this, the affectionate critics are right. The old established church presents numerous difficulties because it is encrusted with tradition and weighted down with the burden of nominal membership. Whereas, in the Church of the Saviour, the normal attendance at a public meeting far exceeds the membership, the situation is reversed in the ordinary established church.

In the light of this observation we must ask what those in old established congregations can do, once they have read this book and believed its message. The answer is that most of them must start where they are. This story was not written in the hope of creating exact copies of what is happening in one congregation in the nation's capital. It was written, instead, to encourage Christian people to start new growths within existing structures or outside them. Gordon Cosby knows very well that the task of renewing the Church of Christ is not easy and that there is no single pattern of renewal, but he is convinced that integrity of membership is the place to begin. The story which this book records gives ample evidence that this judgment is correct.

The story of the Church of the Saviour is a very disturbing story. It makes most of us ashamed of our mild Christianity. We cannot merely read this book, admire it, and forget it. We must either reject it or alter our lives, for this book is a criticism. It is a

criticism couched, not primarily in words, but in events. There
are, at one point on this earth, men and women who have been so
touched by the love of Christ that they tithe their time as well as
their money, make their secular occupations into ministries, and
pray and study and witness and serve. These same people have
avoided spiritual pride by virtue of the fact that their standard
is so high they never reach it. They are daily conscious of the contrast between their standard and their practice.

The story has been told before, in a fragmentary way, but now
it is fully told and for this we can be thankful. I am glad that there
was no hurry. The demonstration has now been going on long
enough to make us reasonably sure that it will endure. Already the
demonstration has borne good fruit in hundreds of communities
where people are given new hope of what a committed fellowship
of Christians might be. Now, with the publication of this book, a
new chapter in the growth of its influence will begin. Accordingly
I thank God and take courage.

PREFACE

This is the story of the Church of the Saviour in Washington, D. C., by one of its members. I am certain that each of us who participates in its life would have chosen different events to record what is happening here. No effort is made to tell of the individual witness of this people. The stories which are included are those which came to mind to help tell the corporate story; the pronoun "we" is used throughout the book to refer to the people of the Church of the Saviour. I think that one biographer expressed for all biographers the feeling that attends the end of any account which attempts to speak of God's dealings with us: "But there are also many other things which Jesus did; were every one of them to be written, I suppose that the world itself could not contain the books that would be written" (John 21:25).*

Many persons have had a part in this book. It would not have been undertaken at all without the needed encouragement of the Rev. Robert A. Raines, Yvonne and Robert Smith, and Dorothy Ham. All through its writing it was held in the prayers of the membership and especially of that little group of intercessors who meet each Wednesday in the church chapel. Lou Longfellow, our meticulous keeper of records, gave precious files into my keeping without a word of instruction, despite my reputation for losing things. Kathryn Campbell gave ungrudgingly of her time to edit

---

* All scripture quotations are from the Revised Standard Version of the Bible unless otherwise noted.

and comment, and wrote several of the course descriptions which appear in Appendix 1. The photographs were taken by Hart Cowperthwait, who is in charge of lighting and photographic exhibits at the Potter's House. Inez Wilkinson not only typed the manuscript as though she had been especially favored, but did much of the work of the church for a number of weeks so that I might be free to write. Thelma Hemker and Louella Stanton answered telephones and fixed meals and did all those things which help to make easier the writing of a book. Alma Newitt was a gentle and perceptive critic. To these and many others I acknowledge my indebtedness.

I would especially express my gratitude for Gordon Cosby, who has been friend and pastor, and in whose life I first saw the gospel. Many pages of this book draw heavily upon his sermons and class material, though this has not always been indicated.

Finally, I would mention my deep indebtedness to the members of the Church of the Saviour, who have also been friends and pastors and in whose company I walk toward a new land.

E.O'C.

Call

to

Commitment

1 *God Calls a People*

The brownstone house in Washington, D. C. that has looked on so much of our life together has a small brass plaque to the left of its door. It reads:

HEADQUARTERS OF
THE CHURCH OF THE SAVIOUR

Strangers read it and ask if we have other churches in other cities or if we plan to start a new denomination. To those of us who worship here on a Sunday morning, the sign is a reminder that we are also the church during all the hours of the week—in the neighborhoods where we live, in our homes, in offices and factories—for "the place whereon you stand is holy ground." We did not know on the day that sign went up what forms the church would take, but we did know that it would exist not only in a building.

Small, wiry Lizzie Simmons is the one who keeps the brass plaque polished. Lizzie was the housekeeper of the rooming house that was our first building. She likes to explain to visitors that we bought her with the house. Except for the words on the sign and a few others, Lizzie has never learned to read or write, but hers is the wisdom of those who have been instructed by the spirit of Christ. When we get out of hand Lizzie threatens to leave; however, this is strictly according to New Testament teaching which says one must admonish a brother.

Lizzie also keeps the high polish on all the floors of this old Victorian mansion. The polished floors belong to the light, airy beauty which is part of the house. To walk through its doors into the paneled, high-ceilinged rooms is to come upon a people—perhaps to touch a Life.

There is a mystic wind that blows across our days. Tomorrow it may be different, but now you hear the sound of it. You hear it in lives that are being changed—sometimes suddenly and dramatically, sometimes slowly and painfully. On a Sunday morning a committed atheist and a committed alcoholic listen to the same sermon and their ways are made radically different. In the years to come these widely variant personalities will many times sit down together and find rest in the company of each other. Here the shy learn how to speak with eloquence, the fearful know courage, the prejudiced Negro and white call one another "brother." The fatherless find a father and the wounded a physician.

The wind blows and you hear the sound of it in the diversity of temperaments that makes up this people and marks each one an individual in the mosaic window that is a fellowship. No sameness dulls the fabric of the life we have together. A hundred different hues make up the pattern. We have learned that our very uncommonness is the gift we bring to one another; the lamb and the lion do lie down together.

The wind blows and you hear the sound in the many gifts that give expression to our days. A few come with ten talents and some with one, but almost all come with their little gifts clutched in tight fists, having said somewhere in secret, "I will use my talent in this way and in that way for this gain and for that gain—always with caution lest I be without in the day of need that will come." Hugging talents, hugging possessions, hugging ourselves to ourselves until we learn that the winds that blow here are the winds of God, that Christ is the breath of life, and that we perish if we hold that breath. Tasks become gifts that enable us to enter into the incarnate life of Christ, who will make us apostles to the city in which we are set.

The wind blows and you hear the sound thereof in a coffee house when Esther Dorsey explains to a seminary student the philosophy of evangelism which undergirds this effort; the man delivering pies overhears, and is so excited that two hours pass before he leaves.

The same wind blows as we build a retreat lodge, and when at a crucial point, the one professional carpenter among us falls sick, a tall lean man appears in our midst—and all through the week we follow his expert direction. When our own carpenter returns the stranger departs as mysteriously as he came. One man says to another,

"We surely couldn't have got along without your friend. We're so glad that he could come with you."

"*My* friend!" says the other in astonishment. "We all thought that he was your friend and that he came with you."

Out of the woods there comes a tall lean man to tarry with us a week, and the wind blows through the trees of the forest where we hammer and saw and build a house which we call the Lodge of the Carpenter. It blows as we build an amphitheater, and then a camping area, as we plow and till the soil and learn in our meeting with earth and rock and one another who we are and something of what it means to be a people of God in the twentieth century.

That wind blows as we plan a Renewal Center where the emotionally ill can be placed in the center of the Christian community. Here we will provide the best medical help and the best counseling available, but more than this, the prayers of the faithful.

That wind still blows as we fail to do what we see to do, fail to be what we know to be; as we take for granted the gift of fellowship with another Christian and wake to find it lost; as we know forgiveness and learn to forgive; learn that there is pain in growth and that suffering is the portion of our days; as we make friends with sorrow, and discover that if we are to live at all, it must be down at the edges of the world where we can be in the company of Him who has called us.

This is a glimpse of the church in the brownstone house. It had its real beginning in the year 1917 when Newton Gordon Cosby was born into a household which experientially knew what the word "ecumenical" meant. Kathleen Gordon Cosby was a faithful

Presbyterian and Peter Guerrant Cosby a deeply convinced Baptist. Their respect and devotion for each other became the window through which they saw that God does not speak to us all by means of the same forms. When they married they agreed that each would continue to go to his own church; the first child would be raised a Presbyterian, the second a Baptist, the third Presbyterian . . . Five children were born to the Cosbys. According to their covenant the second—Newton Gordon—went with his father to the Baptist church. After this, Guerrant Cosby relinquished his claim to any of the other children, saying,

"Kathleen, I have my hands full with this one Baptist you've given me. You may take the rest with you."

The church where Guerrant Cosby was a deacon, as his fathers before him had been, was the Rivermont Avenue Baptist Church in the then peaceful, tradition-bound town of Lynchburg, Virginia. Every Sunday morning Gordon attended church with his father, but on Sunday night and during the week he accompanied his mother to the Presbyterian church. In these two churches he learned the fundamentals of Christianity. The convictions and the beliefs of the Christian Church were sharply drawn and hammered into a child: "Salvation is by Jesus Christ. . . . You must be born again. . . . The Scriptures have been given directly by God. . . ." They were convictions and beliefs so precisely stated that a person knew what he must do to obey. The nineteenth-century church often conceived its witness in verbal terms alone—a man could by his *words* "win souls for Christ."

Gordon was in his early teens when he first consciously began to engage in evangelism. There was a moving within his spirit which made him know that a person had to make witness to his faith and that it had to be done on a consistent basis. Because he wanted to incorporate this teaching of the church into his own life, he and his brother, P. G., agreed that each day they would talk to one person about salvation. It was a decision that they could not carry through. "We needed to put teeth into it," said Gordon, "and we decided that if either of us missed a single day we would give the other a dollar. This brought in the strong economic motivation which did the job."

Many a night the young evangelist lay in bed, remembering that he had talked to no one that day. Fortunately his room was on the first floor, and he could dress and climb out the window without disturbing the household. The Cosby home was on the edge of town, however, and there were not many souls abroad to be saved at that time of night. Always, though, he could find a person an eighth of a mile from home because that was the end of the street-car line and the motorman had to step out, pull down one trolley, and let out the other for the return trip. "I would pull out my tract—a little gospel of John—and say, 'I want to talk to you about the Scripture and I want to talk to you about your spiritual life, and whether or not you are a Christian.' "

Gordon soon discovered that motormen, at least, feel threatened by this kind of approach. While something in him confirmed that he had a priceless gospel which must be shared, and shared on a consistent basis, he began to wonder about his method of communication.

The evangelistic zeal implanted in the mind and heart of young Gordon Cosby was to deepen and change its emphases in the coming years without any lessening of youthful enthusiasm. Books and teachings which departed from his early instruction and experience simply challenged his thinking and broadened his concept of the church and its mission. He could question precepts and forms and methods without shaking the foundations of his life because those foundations rested not on words or forms but on the Author of them. A life firmly rooted in God was the priceless heritage of his boyhood home.

More than any other quality this willingness to question, and when necessary to give up the old and embrace the new, was to characterize his ministry. It was a flexibility of spirit that had been nurtured by parents who gave to their children freedom to engage in all kinds of adventures and projects. Guerrant Cosby had chosen for his homesite eight acres of land so that his children would have space in which to grow and to experiment with whatever caught their imaginations. Though he never picked up the pieces when something failed, he was always there himself to lend support. Kathleen Cosby watched over her fold in a different way. A deep stability characterized her own life, and her children could count on her for an ever concerned response. She made it easy for them to believe in a God who was "without variableness or shadow of turning." In their home the Cosby children lived and breathed the meaning of Christian vocation. Instructed by example, they grew up understanding that the first call upon them was to belong to the Body of Christ and to bring to this fellowship whatever gifts they had.

When Gordon was fifteen Dr. Ernest Campbell became the minister of the Rivermont Avenue Baptist Church and moved into the manse with his wife and three children—Elizabeth-Anne, Mary, and Charles. These were the persons with whom Gordon was to share a life and a ministry. Mary, especially, was to be his constant companion.

Dr. Campbell soon put Gordon in charge of the Royal Ambassadors—a group of roughneck little boys who sang with much gusto:

> I am a stranger here within a foreign land;
> My home is far away, upon a golden strand;
> Ambassadors-to-be of realms beyond the sea,
> I'm here on business for my King.

What his charges began to understand as the months went by was that their leader really was on business for his King. The rules of the Royal Ambassadors were too lax for young Gordon, who was beginning to sense that the Army of Christ needed to be a strong, disciplined order. He began to deal with the issue of paper membership as he transmitted to the boys his own evangelistic zeal. Meetings were changed from once a month to once a week. The ranking system of page, knight, and full-fledged royal ambassador was tightened. No boy became a royal ambassador until he had won a man for Christ.

In these months the family in the manse became Gordon's close friends. The boy was drawn by the sincerity and integrity of the new minister, in whom he saw the singleness of vision and gentle ways of a man yoked with Christ. Under Dr. Campbell's direction he had the freedom—now within the church—to use his imagination and abilities. His evangelistic efforts reached into new fields. The dramatic productions of the young people's group did not gain more professionalism under his direction, but they became more original and gathered suspense. If Gordon needed an ally, and he often did, he found it in Mrs. Campbell. Hers was a deeply spiritual nature untamed by organized piety. The church cleaning-staff soon gave up complaining to her about the use of their equipment as theatrical props. Her typical response was, "Which is more important—a mop or a boy's soul?"

Gordon, the Campbell children, and their close friends in the church often gathered in the front room of the Campbell home or around the kitchen table to dream and plan for the church. It seemed to them that Christ often was not at the heart of church attendance. Few of their contemporaries were asking how they might serve Christ. They were at church because their mothers sent them or because there was a boy or girl present whom they wanted to see. The parents were motivated in much the same way. Some went because their parents before them had gone. It had never occurred to them not to go to church. Others went for social reasons, and some because of business reasons or for the feeling of well-being it gave them.

Gordon Cosby along with Elizabeth-Anne and Mary Campbell began to envision a church that would be alive with Christ. Some of the young people meeting with them turned their thoughts to missionary service. Mrs. Campbell, passing through the room, would often stop to inject her words of counsel.

"Some of you," she would say, "have got to stay home and make the same sacrifices as those who go to Indochina and take years to prepare, learning the language, the customs, and such things. You must learn a new language also, the language of the world, so that those who are worldly and sophisticated, but spiritually illiterate, can understand you. You must do everything they do, and do it better—but without sin. Read better and more broadly than they do, entertain better and more charmingly, dress better and have a knowledge of all the things in which they are interested, so that you can understand their point of view. If you do not do this, you will speak not only a foreign language in this pagan country, but one that repels."

Years later when they planned the staff of the church of their dreams they listed: one minister; one social worker; one director of music; one completely committed, deeply spiritual, glamorous party girl. They were serious. The church was to speak the language of the pagan world it was to win—to say in the language of that world, "Brother, are you saved?"

Beauty and loveliness were to be part of that church because Mary Campbell recalled church suppers in the basement of the recreation hall, where paper cloths had been laid over sawhorses and planks; where flowers had been thrust into bottles discolored by the stainings of many waters; where unshaded forty-watt bulbs had dangled on cords from the ceiling. She had contrasted those dinners with ones she saw in movies. The screen dinners were always by candlelight. The water was served in long-stemmed glasses with clinking ice. There was a sparkle about everything, and in the background soft music played. It had seemed strange to her that the church represented its life by drabness, and hoped to win a world which had appropriated color and light. The church they dreamed of would have order and beauty because God was order and beauty.

It never occurred to the young people that it would be other than a Baptist church. All their dreams had been attached to the conventional, established church. This was the church they had been born into, and grown up to love.

Gordon's first call to preach came when he was fifteen. He and his brother, P. G., had been wandering through the backwoods of Lynchburg when they came upon an abandoned two-room church. They inquired of an elderly, distinguished-appearing, gray-haired Negro man, who was passing by, if the church were ever used.

"I'm the chief deacon," the man said, "but we have no minister."

After giving a convincing account of their activities in two churches, they asked,

"How would you like us to be your ministers?"

The chief deacon made no commitment.

"You can come and preach this Sunday," he said.

There were a dozen people—men, women, and children—in that first congregation. Gordon Cosby's text was Rev. 3:15-16: "I know your works; you are neither cold nor hot. Would that you were cold or hot! So, because you are lukewarm, and neither cold nor hot, I will spew you out of my mouth."

The sermon was one that he was to preach again and again in a hundred different ways. Appreciative "Amens" punctuated its first delivery.

A congregation helps make a preacher what he is. Gordon's first congregation loved him, and he in return loved them. The membership grew to forty. For five years he and P. G. served that church. Then they gave the pastorate over into the hands of their younger brothers, who served the church for another four years.

When Gordon informed Mrs. Campbell that he was going to the Southern Baptist Theological Seminary in Louisville, Kentucky, her ready response was,

"There are enough jack-leg preachers now and you haven't been to college."

A conference with seminary authorities convinced them that it was right for him to begin seminary training. After several months at seminary he decided to pursue college work at the same time. In 1942 he was graduated *magna cum laude* from Hampden Sydney College, and in the same year he completed his seminary training and was ordained a Baptist minister. His college and seminary studies had been compressed into four and one-half years. During that time he had also courted Mary Campbell. One week after he was graduated from seminary they were married.

Their first church was the Ballston Baptist Church, situated in a tiny village in Arlington County, Virginia. This church became the focal point of their dreams. It was the church that Gordon

Cosby was serving when he enlisted in the army, and it was the church that he planned to return to when the war was over.

In the Second World War he was to hammer out a concept of churchmanship which would change the direction of his ministry. As chaplain of the 327th Glider Infantry Regiment, 101st Airborne Division, he saw the church from a new vantage point —outside it. It would never have happened if the circumstances of war had not forcibly placed him there. For the first time he was an observer of the church in the world; he was in the position of receiving people who presumably had been trained by the church for a ministry to the world—to be light in the midst of darkness. Yet, these men, who had been in all the training units of the church, were no more ready for a deadly mission than the unchurched. What he observed was "Christian" men who could not stand up under pressure, not even moral pressure. "If they just didn't go to pieces morally, you could feel grateful for that kind of survival." What he had thought was character, he began to know was the structure of family, society, law enforcement agencies. When this was taken away life did not hold together because internally it was not held together.

Spearheading the Normandy invasion, the 101st Airborne was dropped by glider and parachute on the beaches of France, fought its way through Bastogne, and terminated in the army of occupation. Twice Gordon Cosby was awarded the Bronze Star for rescuing wounded men and for joining an assault company within close range of enemy lines. These were months of self-searching and determinative experiences for him.

There was Joe with whom he had talked about the forms of the church. He worked with Joe over a period of time, investing something of himself in the relationship. He baptized Joe into the Christian faith, as he had many other men. Several months later he inquired of Joe's officer,

"Tell me, how is Joe getting along?"

"What do you mean?" said the officer.

"I mean as a Christian. What kind of life is he leading?"

The officer leaned back in his chair and laughed.

"If Joe's a Christian," he said, "nobody in the company knows it."

There are for all of us revelatory moments in which we see ourselves. As a chaplain, Gordon Cosby had to make out a report on the number of conversions and the number of baptisms each week. He wanted his report to compare favorably with the other chaplains'—and he wanted a promotion. After all, he rationalized, he could do more for Christ and His work as a Division Chaplain; and too, the reports were sent to the denominational representative, who could influence his future. In the case of Joe he saw himself conforming to the world's standard of success; putting first the praise of men. On that day Gordon Cosby was through forever with paper membership; he began to ponder how to assure the integrity of belonging to the Body of Christ.

There were other concerns. How does the chaplain of a regiment best serve three thousand men who are facing the exigencies of life and death? It was impossible to do the job that needed to be done. The sheer necessity of the moment gave birth to what we now know was the forerunner of the fellowship and mission groups in the Church of the Saviour. He chose the most spiritually mature man in each company to be the sky pilot. Around each of the twelve sky pilots was a little nucleus of men who were responsible for the spiritual development of others in their company. Unofficially the companies were known as the Airborne Christian Church. The extraordinary happened in those little bands. A new, contagious life possessed them, so that each company added daily to its number. Soon they outgrew their English chapel and had to move into a gymnasium for worship services.

The demands of wartime were shaping the ministry of Gordon Cosby because they were letting him see himself against the backdrop of eternity. A few days after the Normandy invasion they were to make the first serious assault into enemy lines. It was to take place at two o'clock in the morning. They were to cross a little river and take a hill. The assignment was dangerous enough for them to realize that half their number would die. Gordon decided that the best thing for him to do was to visit with as many of the men as he could in the moments before the assault. It was a cold, drizzly night, though it was June, and he could not see the faces of the men with whom he talked. Crawling into one of the fox-holes, he started,

"I'm the Chaplain. Just wanted to talk to you a bit."

"I'm glad you're here," returned the soldier. "I wanted to talk to you. I have a premonition that I am going to die tonight—that I will meet God before the night is over, and I don't know Him. I want you to talk to me about Him." And then he added, "Don't give me any stuff about philosophy or theology. I just want you to talk to me about God."

In that moment the young chaplain discovered that he did not know nearly so much about God as he had five minutes before. He did not know what to say. Uneasiness filled him, but within a few seconds he found himself saying,

"I would like to talk to you about a verse of Scripture which means a lot to me: 'For God so loved the world . . .' "

He talked to the soldier as simply as he knew about those words of Scripture.

The next morning he checked the casualty list. The man was dead. "I wondered about him," Gordon recalls. "He had been so close to me, and I wondered how those last words had hindered or helped him now that he was in the presence of God. Then it occurred to me that this man was every man. What difference does it make whether it is two hours, or two years, or twenty years. Every man is going to be in the presence of God one day, and every man is crying out, 'Speak to me of things which are eternal. Speak to me of God.' "

In moments like these he knew that he would be the minister of a congregation at home with the great words of the faith—God, Christ, Holy Spirit, grace, forgiveness.

The little Baptist church from which he was on leave wrote that they had the opportunity to have a minister and felt the need of it. Gordon Cosby sent his resignation, feeling that God was directing him to something new. There had taken shape in his mind basic convictions of churchmanship, which he felt could not be expressed

within the church as it was then. War had taught him that if one
is to live meaningfully under stress over an extended period of time,
he must find a deep reality in religion. It is all-important that one
know God for oneself. All else is secondary. Gordon wanted to be
free to experiment—to try to build a church wherein the members
would be committed to Christ and committed to one another in
unlimited liability. In such a fellowship the Holy Spirit could dwell
and give to men firsthand knowledge of God.

The church he dreamed of would be ecumenical: It would work
and pray for the healing of the divisions between all churches. He
felt the call on his own life as he sat around campfires with men
of different religious backgrounds and they shared with one another
the life they had in Christ. Denominational lines as he had known
them seemed more and more artificial. "We discovered that no one
had all the truth. Each of us had a part—maybe an important part,
but only a part. We found that the best way to retain this truth
that meant much to us was to share it with others—to keep it by
giving it away. There was a richness in this diverse fellowship that
we had never known before. As we interpreted our own faith to
those of different denominational backgrounds, the fellowship became alive and creative. New notes were added; the symphony
came to be more God's music. Again and again our talk turned to
how we would invest our lives, if and when we were allowed
to return to the States."

The church he dreamed of would know that its mission was to
take a world for Christ. In this alone there would be unity. Wartime had taught him also that when attention is focused on an
all-important objective, minor differences and irritations slip
away, petty rivalries are forgotten. Maybe you did not like the
person manning an installation. You did not approve of his standards; you did not appreciate his language; you certainly did
not care for his table manners. But those things, in the face of the
common task when a cause was endangered, melted into insignifi-
cance. Every man was playing a vital part in the winning of a
battle, and you were grateful for him. Gordon wrote to Mary: "The
task of spiritual reconstruction and rehabilitation that confronts us

makes the Battle of the Bulge appear in contrast like a Boy Scout Jamboree. When we conceive the proportions of the battle that will take a world for Christ, then on that day we shall be already one. In recognition of our need, we shall belong to one another."

Between battles of the Second World War, he wrote, with the encouragement and inspiration of new friends, the first prospectus of the Church of the Saviour and mailed it home to Mary and Elizabeth-Anne. His covering letter explained that he was not sure that this was their calling, but that he was leaning in the direction of a church which would welcome into its membership persons of any denomination. Its mission, however, would be the quarter of a million unchurched in the capital city of the United States.

Evangelism was basic to Gordon Cosby's thinking, and another letter home explained that if each member were truly committed and won two other members to Christ each year, and always two won two, within twenty-five years not only Washington, D. C., but the whole world would be won for Christ. Sheets of statistics were enclosed to substantiate the statement. It was all very thrilling because it seemed all very possible. Slowly he learned that it was not to happen this way. Faith is not the task of ten or twenty or thirty years, but of a lifetime, and blessed are they who endure to the end. "Strait is the gate and narrow is the way" (Matt. 7:14a, AV).

Mary and Elizabeth-Anne felt called to the same adventure and when Gordon came home they began to plan for it. They asked their friends who knew God to pray in a disciplined fashion concerning the wisdom and rightness of bringing into existence such a church in Washington, D. C. Their friends did—people in England, France, and Holland as well as in twenty-five states. As they prayed, most of them felt a oneness in the thrill of certainty that this was God's will. Throughout that first year over one hundred friends were kept in touch with progress made. These persons continually prayed for members and for the power and spirit the pioneers would have to have.

That first summer after Gordon's return, he and Mary spent much time talking to Christian leaders, asking for their reactions to the spirit, plans, and direction of the Church of the Saviour.

Elizabeth-Anne wrote a new prospectus from a maze of dreams about the yet unborn church. This was freely distributed to any who might be interested. Dr. Campbell, then minister of the First Baptist Church in Alexandria, Virginia, and Mrs. Campbell encouraged several couples in their church to meet with the new group. Among them were Dorothy and Frank Cresswell. Dorothy was a Baptist and Frank a Methodist, and they had continued in the different denominations after their marriage. In the Church of the Saviour they could both belong to the same congregation. The other couples were the Bryans and the Knapps. Neither of the men in these families was interested in church, but it seemed to them as though they might be able to help "these visionaries." The group also found their "deeply spiritual, glamorous party girl" through Dr. and Mrs. Campbell. After a tour of duty ferrying planes for the WASPS, Ellen Wimberly happened to be in Alexandria for a short time and visited Dr. Campbell's church one Sunday. When she learned there of the plans for the new church, Ellen was certain her destiny belonged with it. Although her work took her to Hawaii for a year, she continually upheld the group through her prayers and tithes and later returned to become social director and later still Mrs. Charles Campbell.

Elizabeth-Anne, a student nurse at Garfield Memorial Hospital in Washington, was carrying on her own evangelistic program for the new church. One day she walked into the office of the director of nurses and asked permission to help initiate a weekly period of worship for the student body of the hospital. It was arranged, and soon afterward Gordon Cosby held the first vesper service for Garfield nurses. Girls affiliating at St. Elizabeth's Hospital, also in Washington, asked for similar services. Countless hours were spent in conferences, informal bull sessions, and visits by members of the group with members of the hospital families. In preparation for the services, a tiny group of nurses, some of whom were new Christians, fasted and prayed. The nurses of Garfield and St. Elizabeth's were well represented among the first members of the Church of the Saviour.

In the meantime the initial group, which had grown to twelve,

held its own worship service at 4:00 P.M. on Sunday in a borrowed
church building. Afterward they would adjourn to a home or to
one of Washington's restaurants for dinner. The conversation always led them to discuss Christianity as it was related to their
varied and busy lives and to the life of the world. Others began to
find the group exciting and asked to meet with it. Those who
expressed an interest in becoming members of the church were led
in weekly studies in which the plan and price of Christian living
were taught. They were the first students in what was to be known
as the School of Christian Living.

As a program of evangelism went forward, the group bent its
efforts to raise money. They wrote to everyone they had ever
known and to several philanthropists who came to their attention.
At that time the word "ecumenicity" was little used, and when
John D. Rockefeller, Jr., published an article on the subject, they
confidently felt it was God pointing out His man. They wrote
immediately to Rockefeller describing the scope and spirit of their
plan and asking if a single church on the local level could be
ecumenical or was the word used only in reference to the larger
movement. They also explained that the members of their group
were comparatively young and that while they were ready to invest
their lives, they did not have financial strength to launch their
program on the scale that was so desperately needed. "We are praying for someone who will provide a building to serve as headquarters."

Rockefeller sent back a warm and friendly letter expressing
genuine interest but stating firmly that time and strength would
not permit him the satisfaction of even a distant consultative relationship to the undertaking.

The group was greatly encouraged and again wrote, and again
received a friendly letter. Finally Gordon wrote: "I know that such
things as this only happen in fairy tales, but I shall be in New York
on Thursday and if by chance you will see me for a few minutes, I
will come to the 56th floor of Rockefeller Plaza. I will value your
time."

The answer came in a telegram:

YOUR LETTER TO MR. ROCKEFELLER, JR., RECEIVED. WHILE MR.
ROCKEFELLER CANNOT SEE YOU HIMSELF WHEN YOU ARE IN NEW
YORK TOMORROW HIS ASSOCIATE MR. PACKARD WILL BE GLAD TO
SEE YOU IN MR. ROCKEFELLERS OFFICE ON THE 56TH FLOOR.
PLEASE WIRE ME COLLECT WHEN YOU PLAN TO CALL.

Mary opened the telegram and immediately telephoned Elizabeth-Anne at Garfield. "Put on your best black dress. We're going
to New York to receive our inheritance!"

Undergirded by the prayers of their tiny group, Gordon, Mary,
and Elizabeth-Anne left for New York. In joyful anticipation they
spent the night in a luxury hotel. The following morning Gordon
went to the 56th floor of 30 Rockefeller Plaza while Mary and
Elizabeth-Anne ordered scrambled eggs in a restaurant from which
they could watch the ice skaters. They sat close to the telephone
booth and propped the door open with a jar of nail polish so that
they could hear it ring when Gordon called to say that it was time
for them to join him and be presented. Gordon was gone a very long
time but the phone never rang. Eventually they saw him walking
through the doorway of the restaurant, smiling sadly and shaking
his head. Elizabeth-Anne reports that Mary's tears dropped into her
scrambled eggs and that with her fork she stirred tears and eggs
together. It had never occurred to any of them that Rockefeller
would wire them to come in order to refuse their request.

They had envisioned the church as an endowed church because
they resented the church of Christ having to beg for money. They
wanted to be able to say, "Come, this is for you." Two years later
when Mary watched Bob Knapp staining the floor of the chapel of
their first building at three o'clock in the morning, she knew how
wrong they had been. The church belonged to them all in the deep
way that it did because of the terrible sacrifices of giving that had
been made. They had given of time and sleep and possessions.

The first official meeting of the Church of the Saviour took place
on a Saturday afternoon, October 5, 1946, at the First Baptist
Church, Alexandria. The constitution and directory of church

order were discussed at the meeting, but it was decided by the group that church incorporation should wait until there were more financially responsible members. This was one of the ideas they later had to give up, since it became apparent that it would be years before any of them would be considered by the world "financially responsible."

The constitution of the church as outlined at the first meeting stated that

the Church of the Saviour will endeavor to enter into full fellowship and cooperation with all Christian groups and denominations. It will seek a close relationship and affiliation, where possible, with all organizations and movements representing united or cooperating Christian churches, such as the local council and the National Council of Churches. It will seek to be subject to the will of the universal Church in so far as this will be expressed by such representatives and organizations. In particular, it will seek to promote, to be in association and fellowship with, and to be subject to the World Council of Churches as the representation and expression of Christianity throughout the world.

The Church of the Saviour is to be regarded as a part or unit of Christ's Church, with a distinctive ecumenical spirit and approach, allowing freedom of worship, practice and belief among its own constituents, while remaining true to the basic values in the stream of historic evangelical Christianity; attempting to bear a unique witness of spiritual power, while at the same time recognizing the validity, the integrity and the rights of self-determination of all Christian groups and denominations. It is considered, however, that an obligation rests upon all such groups and denominations to surrender to the sovereignty and will of Christ as these are expressed through the voice of the ecumenical Church in our day.

Over the next weeks the group, under the direction of P. G., who was now a Presbyterian clergyman, worked out the constitution in detail, covering membership, finances, and government.

It was during the third meeting that the group decided it must have a place of its own in which to gather, and a motion was carried that a building fund be established. Thirty dollars was subscribed that night. It stood at this figure for a number of months, but by April $2,500 had been accumulated. By then the group had inspected numerous buildings, which Providence kindly did not permit them to acquire. On a rainy, cold day in March the real estate committee stumbled on a dark, run-down rooming house and knew that they had to have it. Each member of the group who went to consider the purchase walked through the house with mounting enthusiasm. The gray stone building at 1707-19th Street, with its arched windows, began to look more and more like a church to them.

The price was reasonable—$28,000 in addition to a down payment of $5,000. This included the furniture and the roomers, if the new church could keep them. The new church welcomed both the additional income and the roomers, several of whom were to be among its early members. The group dispersed, to borrow on life insurance and from friends and relatives the balance needed to make up the $5,000. The owner was so transported by their enthusiasm that he began to jump from one foot to the other while he exclaimed excitedly that he would like to make a contribution. Again they saw visions of Rockefeller-size donations. Each person held his breath in anticipation as the new-found benefactor magnanimously announced that his contribution would be five dollars.

In the spring and summer months the four-story building was transformed room by room. Floors were scraped and varnished, furniture re-upholstered, and draperies made. Old rugs were scrubbed and restored to lovely shades by mixing dye in detergent. Rooms were plastered and repainted, and book shelves and altars built. The one person employed by the work parties was an alcoholic who had to be sobered up each day. At night they would say to him,

"Edward, come back tomorrow. We have no paint, but come anyway."

In the morning mail would be the five or ten dollars they needed to carry on the work of another day. Most of the contributions came from Gordon's war buddies, who were kept informed of the progress in the old house.

The largest room was made into a chapel, and the others into offices, classrooms, a library, a reception hall, and a dining room.

The roomers on the fourth floor were early caught up in the work and lived in a perpetual house party. Tendrils of wisteria were painted along the cracks in rooms that seemed beyond repair. On the walls of the ecumenical room were painted wide oceans and scenes from all over the world. On every other possible wall artists painted landscapes. The reception room was a cool green with murals of cherry orchards, fields, and seascapes. Even the furnace room had its special decor of brightest yellow with Peter Hunt decorations covering the furnace. Endless energy, imagination, and enthusiasm accompanied the work of every room, and a boundless, contagious joy.

In the midst of this intense activity Gordon received an invitation to speak at the National Convention of Community Churches, which was to take place in Chicago. The subject sent him by the planning committee was "The New Ecumenical Church in Our Nation's Capital." The work parties, awed and humbled, redoubled their efforts.

Finally, in October, the work was completed. At three o'clock in the morning of October 19, 1947, the last floor was stained, the last paint stroke completed. The place stood in readiness.

That afternoon at four o'clock the first service was held in the chapel, which was filled to overflowing. Nine people stood and repeated the commitment of membership:

I come today to join a local expression of the Church, which is the body of those on whom the call of God rests to witness to the grace and truth of God.

I recognize that the function of the Church is to glorify God in adoration and sacrificial service, and to be God's missionary to the world, bearing witness to God's redeeming grace in Jesus Christ.

I believe as did Peter that Jesus is the Christ, the Son of the Living God.

I unreservedly and with abandon commit my life and destiny to Christ, promising to give Him a practical priority in all the affairs of life. I will seek first the Kingdom of God and His Righteousness.

I commit myself, regardless of the expenditures of time, energy, and money to becoming an informed, mature Christian.

I believe that God is the total owner of my life and resources. I give

God the throne in relation to the material aspect of my life. God is the owner. I am the ower. Because God is a lavish giver I too shall be lavish and cheerful in my regular gifts.

I will seek to be Christian in all relations with my fellowman, with other nations, groups, classes, and races.

I will seek to bring every phase of my life under the Lordship of Christ.

When I move from this place I will join some other expression of the Christian Church.

The nine who were received into membership were Gordon and Mary Cosby, Robert and Martha Knapp, Frank and Dorothy Cresswell, Elizabeth-Anne Campbell, Rosalie Grenier, and Esther Zeller.

The brochure on the new church warned,

This is a dangerous book about a demanding way of life and a vigorous institution that would propagate it. It is dangerous because you may find yourself digging with a shovel, or tracing current theologies, or reading the Bible, or changing your job, or explaining what the word "ecumenism" means or praying as you've never prayed before. It is indeed dangerous, for if one becomes committed to this way, all life will be different and every sphere of one's existence involved in the change.

They were prophetic words, as life after life was to prove. One of the first mission outreaches of the Church of the Saviour was work with teen-agers at the Lily Ponds Housing Development. It was under the direction of a young woman who had come to the new church—herself a teen-age delinquent.

A School of Christian Living was set up, which offered the classes required for membership. There was no kitchen in the building, but a hot meal brought from a nearby cafeteria was a part of the evening class session. The classes were over at 9:30 P.M. but it was always close to midnight before the last person left. No dream was too big to be considered. The members followed the Great Adventurer. They believed they were in on the most important thing in life, and to others they easily transmitted their wonder.

After two years in the house, the church began to think in terms of larger quarters. Sunday after Sunday the little chapel overflowed and people sat on the stairs. The membership now numbered nineteen, but there were many more who were exploring with them the Christian faith. Average income per capita was about $200 per month. Again, as earlier, the financial basis for the proposed move would have horrified most church-building committees. Nevertheless, a group was appointed to look for a suitable building, and the congregation once more devoted itself to a prayerful consideration of its resources. The result was that when a twenty-five-room Victorian mansion at 2025 Massachusetts Avenue was offered for sale on February 20, 1950, for $60,000 cash, the congregation had accumulated $15,000, on the basis of which it was possible to arrange loans and to make the purchase. The total obligation, including necessary remodeling, amounted to about $90,000.

The following months were like those which had preceded the opening of "1707." The drawing room on the first floor of the old house was remodeled into a chapel, and the heating system had to be modernized. This work was let out to contractors. Everything else required to transform the long-closed and gloomy old building into a place of loveliness was a labor of love. Work parties took over and cleaned, polished, and painted for thousands of man-hours. The amateur artisans were given these instructions: "Every time you dip your paint brush in a paint bucket, or fling a mop of soap suds at that beautiful, dirty, wonderful new church, pray a little prayer. Begin always in a moment of silence. Ask the Master Painter to let you 'tap in' on the secrets of the universe to do this job of His." Several professional artists who were members of the congregation gave unstintingly of their talents. A skilled building craftsman used all his spare time for weeks, directing the painting and plastering. An ungainly old building became a hymn of color and beauty.

The brass sign, moved from "1707," was placed to the left of the door, and on October 22, 1950, the brownstone house was dedicated as the Church of the Saviour, an ecumenical church.

2   *Approach to Integrity of Church Membership*

The Church of the Saviour is an attempt to recover in one local expression of the Church Universal something of the vitality and life, vigor and power of the early Christian community. It was founded on the conviction that the greatest contribution the church can make in any time is in being the church—"a fellowship of reconciled and reconciling men," a community of the Holy Spirit, a people in which Christ dwells, a people who have a newness of life and who are transmitters of this newness.

We understand the Christian Church as the gathering of those who are committed to Christ and to one another in the living of a common life. We are to be pioneers, missionaries, evangelists, teachers, and prophets—representatives of the new humanity. The proclamation of the gospel is not alone for a little official group of people which is called clergy. It is for all who have met the Pioneer and Perfecter of our faith, who know that Christ is on the march. The world may be fearful and anxious and weary, but we are not weighted by that world. We are following One who has unfathomable resources and One who makes them available to us and who says, "You must set new norms for life so that people can see what life can be. This is your task. Your primary vocation is to enter into covenant relationships with others who have also met this Christ—to be that new society into which others can be drawn."

We believe that in Christ we have been confronted by the living, active God of the universe—that His is the name in which there is Life, and it is the only name in which there is Life. So we say, "Jesus is Lord. Jesus is King."

Some will say these are traditional words or they will say, "Surely in this day no one really takes them seriously." Our answer is that we do take them seriously. Jesus is King of our congregation; He is King of our individual lives. We are committed to Him for time and eternity. The belonging we have to Christ and to one another deepens our belonging to the church of Christ wherever it is. In many places that church confesses that it is sick and longing for something different. All over the world the church is speaking of its renewal. This is a time when at a deeper level than for many decades the church is trying to discover her own true nature— what it is to be the church of Christ. This asking, seeking, questing, open, repentant church is the church that God will surely use to do in our day a new thing.

The foregoing thoughts remain for us and every church wishful thinking unless we are willing to cope realistically with the issue of entrance into the Christian Church. The current easy access to membership is disturbing to many thoughtful Christians, some of whom are ministers of "successful" churches, where plans are made, programs projected and projects adopted, which though in themselves worthy, do not serve the reconciling purpose. They become ends in themselves. Then people must be won to make possible the continuance of these programs rather than to enter a new life.

Once in a while in the Church of the Saviour we find ourselves thinking, "Now we ought to get hold of this person because he would be just right to help us with some project." This is a dangerous feeling. We never need people simply to help us with a task which we have to do.

The Christian Church has a secret at her heart and the only call upon her is to share it. Whenever by repentance and forgiveness one enters into the community of grace, he discovers the very end of life. Another person is then the possessor of the news that must be told, and must run to find a housetop from which to proclaim it. Thrilling, costly projects come into existence in this way, but not as ends in themselves. People must never become means to an end. In too many worthy enterprises people serve faithfully, yet do not become aware of their own deep need for the acceptance and love which Christ offers, and which will enable them to give such acceptance and love to others.

There are many young ministers today who have inherited that which they feel they cannot perpetuate. They find an overemphasis on organization, but do not know how to change it. Resentment and love are intermingled. They love the church which has given them what they most treasure. At the same time they resent the restrictions that keep them from expressing the leading of the Holy Spirit. Many of them are saying, "If I cannot find more meaning in the church, I will have to leave."

The refusal to grapple with the issue of entrance into the Christian Church is not tolerance; it is betrayal of the gospel which we preach. No one claims that seeking to ensure integrity of membership is not fraught with danger and difficulty, but the answer does not lie in skirting the problem. The profound meanings of membership need to be rethought.

Surely entrance into the Christian Church presupposes total commitment to Christ as the Lord of the church. A surrender to Christ is a surrender to His people—total involvement in the life of the church and the awareness that participation in this community of forgiveness and love means that we must extend it to all mankind.

If the church is to move toward integrity of membership, a framework must be provided prior to membership in which the Christian faith may be explored with seriousness. Within this framework a person must have the opportunity to know deep person-to-person relationships. He must have opportunity in a community of acceptance and love to see himself, to let go his false saviours that he may come to know the real Saviour.

For the Church of the Saviour this framework is the School of Christian Living, which offers the six courses required for membership in the church as well as elective studies for persons already members. The required courses are considered basic to an understanding of the Christian faith, while the elective courses are designed primarily to give members additional opportunity for structured study in special fields. Elective courses have included Interpretative Speech, Counseling, the Christian Classics, History of the Church, Prayer, and Group Dynamics.

This is a typical schedule for a school year:

The School of Christian Living

	Fall Sept.-Jan.	Winter Jan.-April	Spring April-June
Required Courses:*	Old Testament Doctrine Stewardship	New Testament Old Testament Christian Growth	Ethics New Testament Stewardship
Elective Courses:	Prayer	Conducting Retreats	Creative Expression

The educational plan of the church was conceived to explain to the person with little or no church background the Christian Way. The idea was to outline the Truth which had been found unshakable by Christians through the ages.

For the individual student, no creed or theological dogma is memorized, to be glibly recited; rather the student is presented, in present-day terminology, the laws of the spirit as taught by Jesus. He is urged to disprove them if he can, but in any case to try them. The point is especially emphasized that, rather than blindly accepting the claim that Jesus is the Son of the Living God or flatly denying it, the student is to try living with Him for six months.

Rarely is the same course offered twice in the same way, which has made it difficult for us to be helpful to other churches at the

---

* Descriptions of required courses appear in Appendix I.

point of outlines and a syllabus. Various members teach from time to time, which makes for variation in presentation and material used. But even when the same course is taught over and over again by the same person, it is a different course each time. The basic essentials are the same, but the teachers are growing, creative, experimenting people, and so the courses grow and change. What is important in any School of Christian Living is that we present the unmistakable implications of deep and total commitment involved in following Christ—the challenge and risk and danger, the promise and the cost.

The content will always be unimportant alongside the experience of Christ himself. This is why the courses are offered within the context of the Christian community, which is dependent on the inpouring of God's spirit. The community keeps prayerful watch over a newcomer, to listen to him and to understand and encourage him. It is concerned with all the needs of a person. Not only does a person gain new intellectual understanding, but it is hoped he will experience confrontation with the living God. Each course is planned to lead to that most decisive of all choices: total commitment to Christ.

Everyone who enrolls in a class is expected to attend regularly and punctually and to perform faithfully all requirements. Those who wish to audit a class must have the permission of the instructor. Seekers after pleasant parleys have been warned that they will be disappointed.

Most of the participants have attended Sunday worship for three or more months before they enroll in the School, but often the classes have been an introduction to the Christian Church. When we describe the classes they sound formal, solemn, and serious. There is deep seriousness of purpose, but the evening itself is characterized by the color and drama of a festival. It is an evening contagious with the excitement of an expectant people. It was once recorded in these words:

What is a typical evening at our Church? There are some who say that first a banquet is held, with candlelight and the music of many voices sounding as a prelude to a long awaited time. To pause and hear the separate notes is to learn that you are in the company of believers—the fellowship of the forgiven—the gift-bearing community that holds in its hands the gift of life, and has gathered to celebrate and to share that which it has found. They say that He who is the Lord of Life moves amongst them—just as it must have been at a feast in Cana long ago. Whoever will come is welcome here, and when you shut your eyes the tables flash upon the inward sight, and reach to the ends of the earth. Some there are who say this. . . .

And more than this they say. When the banquet tables are rolled away, there follows a time that wraps within its span all that has been, and is, and will be—the community of believers kneels to worship with those who have gone before and those who will come after. No separate note is sounded now. He who loses his life finds it. What was seen in a mirror dimly is revealed face to face. The horizons of the world wait to be pushed back—the infinite Life with the finite to meet. Some there are who say this. . . .

And more than this they say. A command is heard, "Thou shalt love the Lord thy God . . . with all thy mind." To obey is to enroll in a pilgrimage of discovery—the discovery of God, and of man, and of self. It is to find within the pages of a Book the knowledge that makes foolish the wisdom of the world. It is to understand the gifts that God bestows. It is to have all the days for a classroom and the Spirit of Truth for an instructor. Some there are who say this. . . .

And more than this they say. Eternity records the night.

Such is the mystical description of a typical night. The more prosaic say that the evening begins at 6:45 when dinner is served in our wood-paneled dining room. Nowhere is there any evidence of the bare electric-light 40-watt bulbs that Mary remembers from her childhood. The dinner hour is an integral part of a program of evangelism. If we want to bring a friend for the first time, we often telephone ahead so that the friend can be seated with people we feel can best minister to him, but we are learning not to worry when our best-laid plans go astray. A certain sophisticated stranger, whom we were trying hard to win for the kingdom, finally came to the School one night. While our backs were turned, he was seated with a group too enwrapped in their conversation to do much more than acknowledge his arrival. They talked about what God had done for them and introduced one or two sentences with, "God said to me . . ." Some of us ate our meals anxiously, fearing that our new friend would be offended. When the supper was over he rushed up to us and said,

"I've had the most astounding hour of my life! I feel like a kid again. I've got that feeling that life is good."

We still believe in intentional evangelism, but not as completely as we once did. Many of us are past that time when we are sure that we know what is good for a person and who can best be his minister. We now know that God calls his own and that he sometimes uses the most unlikely people.

Our suppers, which are attended by fifty or more, are prepared by participants in the School who take turns and help make it a festive time. Acoustic tile has been installed on the ceiling of the dining area, but nothing stills the sound of many voices exchanging experiences and discussing religious questions: "Why do the good suffer and the wicked prosper?" "Does prayer really work?" "How does one know the will of God?" "What does it mean to be Christian on your job?"

Dinner is followed by a worship period in the chapel, which is led by a member. The classes meet from 8:00 until 9:30. Usually they are limited to twenty members, and when the participants number twelve or less, they seem most effective. This size permits a teacher to shepherd his students and allows members of the class to know each other and to participate in discussions.

God speaks to some in the very first course; for others, the call comes long after all the classes have been completed. Many turn sorrowfully away.

Those who move through the School of Christian Living and feel the call to belong to God and to this particular expression of His church, prepare a short paper which includes:

1. A statement telling what Christ means to the applicant in his personal experience.

2. A statement on his present spiritual discipline, naming those practiced regularly, and for how long. For example: "I am tithing

my full income. For three months I have given 12 per cent of it."

3. A statement on those areas of his life which are obviously unchristian and in which help is needed. For example: Inability to work with others, to belong to others in depth, to handle money, to live out Christ's life in one's home; lack of balance, discretion, or taste; pride; drinking; incontinence in sex. (This is not to suggest that one must be spiritually mature before coming into membership. It does mean, however, that before identifying oneself with a committed membership, the more obvious areas of need should have been lifted to Christ's healing love.)

4. A statement on whatever specific task he is doing for the Church of the Saviour, the length of time he has carried this responsibility, and other work which he feels called to do.

This paper is presented to the Council,* which appoints a sponsor. The call of God that has sounded in the heart of the believer is thus confirmed in the heart of the saving community. The miracle of the imparting of God's life is not likely to have occurred if it is not recognizable to those who have assisted in the pilgrimage. If it is felt that an applicant is not ready for sponsorship, he is appointed a presponsor to help him in his preparation.

The period of sponsorship lasts six weeks or longer. Usually the sponsor and sponsoree meet once a week and study together, following a syllabus which has been prepared as a guide. The commitment is covered line by line and memorized during this time, and the disciplines are discussed one by one. Among the subjects included for discussion are the constitution of the Church of the Saviour, the importance of worship in the life of a Christian, the principle of proportionate giving, and the decentralization of leadership and responsibility so that the membership does not lean on a professional staff to carry on the tasks of the body. Required reading during this period is Dietrich Bonhoeffer's *Life Together*† and at least one book on the Ecumenical Movement, to provide back-

---

* The Council is the governing body of the Church of the Saviour, consisting of two staff members and eight elected representatives.

† New York: Harper & Row, 1954.

ground for a discussion of our relationship to church councils: the local Council of Churches, the National Council, and the World Council.

Again, the relationship between the sponsor and the prospective member is as important as the material covered. Usually the sponsor has been selected because in other situations he has ministered to the prospective member. This is a time when that relationship is deepened and the sponsor has an opportunity in a relaxed, structured time to find out what stage the person has reached in his spiritual life and to help him at the point of his questions or misgivings concerning the step he is about to take. He is in a real sense, though for a limited time, the Spiritual Director of this person.

Almost always the time of sponsorship is one of promise and expectancy, and a time which is joyfully entered into. It sometimes happens, however, that within this period a person faces himself at a deeper level and discovers resistances that he was not aware of until he was actually approaching the hour of commitment. Usually these are worked through, but occasionally the time of joining is put off until a later day.

Bob Smith, who is a political correspondent on Capitol Hill, is one of our members who made the decision to join, but then stepped back for a second look. His doubts were focused in what we call Gordon's Elephant Story. Bob was having dinner at Gordon's table one night during his School of Christian Living days when someone urged Gordon to tell the Elephant Story. It seems that when the circus came to Lynchburg in his teen years, Gordon and several of his friends would climb into an old car and tear off down the back roads. Whenever they saw someone approaching, the car would screech to a halt and Gordon would climb out and breathlessly inquire, "Have you seen an elephant?" The response of "No" brought the explanation that there was a circus in town and one of the elephants was loose. "Keep your eyes open," he would say, "there's a reward." He would then leave instructions on how to catch an elephant and where to deliver it, and depart in a cloud of dust to find the next person. Within a few hours the environs of Lynchburg would be on an elephant hunt.

"This story," said Bob, "convulsed me with laughter. I thought it was one of the funniest stories I had ever heard—perhaps because Gordon was a minister and I didn't expect a minister to be a practical joker. As I neared the end of my preparation for membership and the issue of commitment was facing me, I began to reflect on that story. I began to wonder if this quest I was on hadn't all been conjured up by Gordon Cosby. There was a lot which looked attractive and I wanted it, but on the other hand I began to question if under Gordon's leadership we all weren't following an elephant that wasn't there. Afterward I was to come to know Gordon Cosby better and because of him and others to believe for the first time in my life that it was possible to be a Christian.

"Up until then I thought Christianity was an ideal—a goal to shoot at but not something obtainable. But this came later. Right then I was reasoning that what I needed was an objective point of view. I knew from observing others how easy it is to get caught up in a cause so that your enthusiasm doesn't allow you to properly evaluate where it is leading. I pulled back for that objective look. A trip came along at that time and afforded added perspective. In the next weeks I listened attentively and observed closely those I met. I discovered that everyone had a problem, but these friends didn't have the spiritual resources with which to meet creatively their problems. I couldn't help them because I didn't have them either. I was objective about the church I hopefully described for them, but the price I had paid for objectivity was spiritual inadequacy. I came back to the church knowing that these were the people I wanted to call 'my people.' "

The formal reception into the membership of the Church of the Saviour is on a Sunday morning when a person stands with his sponsor and recites the commitment. Here is formalized what has usually taken place months before. One has become a part of a people with whom the whole of life is bound—a fellowship where all the members are necessary to one another as the eye is to the hand, and as close as, and more intimate than, the members of a family. This is what will mark the church of Christ as different. This is what a spiritually starved world will wonder at: "See how they love one another."

Even the hard world of business will take notice. One of our church members recommended another member for an opening in the office of a business acquaintance. Several years later when a new opening came, the same person inquired about placing another member of the church.

"I'm sorry," said the business friend. "I'm not hiring anyone else from your church."

"Why?" she asked, "I thought Pete was working out fine."

"It's not that," he said. "We make it a policy never to hire two people from the same family and your church is too much of a family."

The other day a man in our coffee house asked, "Who runs this place?" and then added, "Let me guess. It's a family."

We are members now of that family of faith with ties deeper than any we have known before.

This brings us to the issue of continuing and deepening the belonging with Christ and His church, which constitutes the meaning of entrance and membership in the church. Too often the pilgrim on the Christian Way loses sight of the City whose builder and maker is God, and settles down in flat country—a displaced person with no worldly home and no kingdom destiny, the sad-faced refugee of a battle that was to have taken a world for Christ. The cross may be mentioned, but our hearts do not stir. The symbol is dead: the symbol which had the power to interpret our life together, to hold it, to extend it, and to give it new dimensions. We can even hold in our hands broken bread, and we can put to our lips poured-out wine, and nothing burns within our souls. The urgency is lost, the belonging is lost because we were not aware that they could be lost.

The reasons for this may be many, but often it is because we have forgotten that one of our primary responsibilities is the nurturing of our own members. The Christian Church exists to produce saints—God-possessed men and women. More than anything

else it needs to inspire people who are able to transmit the very
life of Christ to other people. This should be one of the real measures of the success of any church. Either we are moving into a
measure of the stature of the fullness of Christ or we are in a time
of retrogression.

This deepening of the spiritual life is not spontaneous. People do
not just become great Christians. They grow as they make certain
purposeful responses to life and to the grace of God. We call these
ordered responses "disciplines." If a discipline does not describe
the nature of the church, it is artificial. For example, if one believes
the church to be a community which lives by prayer, he might well
commit himself to a discipline of daily prayer; if he believes the
church to be a community that lives by giving away its life, he
might adopt a discipline of the giving of money, of time, of service.
If he believes the church lives by the Word of God, he might read
the Bible daily, in order to be open to that Word and to live more
deeply into the community which lives under it.

The following pledge is the present minimum discipline of the
Church of the Saviour.

> We covenant with Christ and one another to:
> Meet God daily in a set time of prayer
> Let God confront us daily through the Scriptures
> Grow in love for the brotherhood and all people, remembering the
>   command, "Love one another as I have loved you"
> Worship weekly—normally with our church
> Be a vital contributing member of one of the groups
> Give proportionately, beginning at a tithe of our incomes
> Confess and ask the help of our fellowship should we fail in these
>   expressions of devotion

We would warn against the disciplines becoming another form
of perfectionism, a holy rule by which one is self-justified. The discipline is a response to the waiting grace of God. It helps keep us
open to the love of God. It helps keep our feet upon the pilgrim
way. He who becomes self-righteous has wrongly conceived the
meaning of the disciplines. Day by day the disciplines let us see our-

selves against the agape love of the cross, and when we thus see ourselves we are led to humility, not pride. As we move toward
God we come for the first time really to know ourselves. In this
movement the concept of self is changing and there is the pain of
self-knowledge. As we see ourselves more clearly, there are new
adjustments to make, new responsibilities to carry. The writer of the
Letter to the Hebrews says: "For the moment all discipline seems
painful rather than pleasant; later it yields the peaceful fruit of
righteousness to those who have been trained by it" (12:11).

To those who earnestly believe that through discipline God gives
freedom and power, we would say several things which might be
helpful in formulating a spiritual discipline:

1. It must be a balanced discipline, relating one properly to the
three major areas of reality—God, persons, and things. Persons relate to God primarily through worship, prayer, and the Scriptures.
Persons relate to persons by love: "Love one another as I have loved
you." Persons relate to things—money, possessions—to the extent
whereby they are not bound by things; not seeking to possess them,
but using them and giving them in the service of God.

2. The disciplines of the spiritual life, to be helpful, must be
specific and definite. All of us are sinful, fallen creatures. The image
of God within man is marred. He needs to know something of the
degree to which he has appropriated the grace available to him. For
instance, instead of adopting a discipline of prayer, it would be
wiser to set aside uncompromisingly fifteen or thirty minutes a day
for that specific purpose. Instead of saying, "I shall give sacrificially," it will be wiser in this discipline to say, "I shall give a proportionate share of my income, the minimum to be not less than 5
or 10 per cent." When one moves from the generalities to the concrete there will be pain, anxiety, pressure, bewilderment. It is when
one becomes specific that he runs into difficulty. One can talk about
the principle of love, but to start applying it often creates a situation of tension and pressure. To speak of growing in the life of
prayer is not difficult, but to start on the Ignatian Way may cause
a person to temper his words.

3. A group should have a graduated discipline. There needs to

be a minimum discipline because it cannot impose on the beginner what is adequate and challenging to those who have been at it for a number of years. Human nature, however, is tempted to adopt the minimum as the maximum. At the Church of the Saviour we are inclined to think of ourselves in terms of a tithing church when we ought to be thinking in terms of proportionate giving. Disciplines should enable one to attain a security so rooted in God that it becomes possible to give more and more. If one begins his prayer life with fifteen minutes of daily prayer and five years later he is still praying only fifteen minutes a day, this fact tells a great deal about the person.

One other thing we would say on the subject of disciplines. One should never encourage another to embrace the disciplines until there is an internal readiness. Sometimes a person wants to adopt disciplines because he feels they will let him belong, let him be a part of the group. If we sense that it is not the fullness of time for a person, we try to discourage it, for there will come the day when he will feel caught in a bind, and will be resistant and hostile. There must be an internal readiness. This is difficult because in a sense there will always be a part of one under pressure, that will not want to pray in the morning. Any ordered response to which we commit ourselves will inevitably cut across the grain of our undisciplined desires. This part of ourselves we can ignore. We do not have to wait for that self to be ready if there is another part of us which knows it cannot live unless it prays.

We discovered how important the disciplines were in a year when we were slacking off. Everyone was talking about disciplines as though they should be forever done away with. Some expressed concern that we were growing legalistic in our practice, but when we discussed this we decided that there were more of us trying to slide through on "cheap grace." We could not find anyone who was so conscientious about the disciplines that we could point a finger and say "legalist." We decided that we were safe, if through the disciplines we were trying to obey those two unlegalistic commandments: "You shall love the Lord your God with all your heart, and with all your soul, and with all your strength, and with all your mind; and your neighbor as yourself" (Luke 10:27).

We also decided that we ought to get rid of any idea we might be entertaining that the disciplines were something we had originated. Basically, they were the classical disciplines practiced through the ages. There may have been variations for different times and situations, but always where the church was vital they had been a part of its life.

When our membership confronted the issue of whether to relax its disciplines, it gave a unanimous "No." At a members' meeting everyone had an opportunity to speak on the subject. Statements varied, but through each shone one unvarying thought: "I need the disciplines for my growth." A three-week discussion ended with the adding of a seventh discipline, which is "to confess and ask the help of our fellowship should we fail in these expressions of devotion."

Even when the gift of discipline has been granted to us there is another hurdle which is exceedingly difficult. A medieval monk stated the law this way: "Discipline begets abundance. Abundance, unless we use utmost care, destroys discipline. Discipline in its fall pulls down with it abundance."

This is the precarious position in which we now find ourselves. Even our present level of commitment and discipline has brought great vitality and astounding abundance. What do we do now with our abundance? Do we give it back to the God who gave it? Do we give it back with the ease with which we brought him our initial poverty?

In the structure of the Church of the Saviour was included a discipline to keep all the other disciplines alive. It is the principle of recommitment: "Each year, under God, we will review our commitment to this expression of the Church. If we find at any time this doesn't have meaning for us or we are automatically performing a ritual, we will not recommit."

And so in October of each year our members affirm anew that we belong to Christ and to one another. The period before recom-

mitment is a time of re-examination, a time when we decide what
our most basic belonging means after another year of pilgrimage.
Are our roots deeper in God's life? Does the common life which we
know in Christ mean more to us than a year ago? Are we willing
to give ourselves to the fellowship at greater cost?

Or is it true that Christ and his ministry mean less as more and
more areas of loneliness and uncertainty and uneasiness have been
satisfied? Do we toy now with conventional structures, which will
be less pressing and less demanding and less revealing, and in which
we can settle down more easily?

Do the people who are called by Christ and redeemed by Him
seem more ordinary than in the first months of wonderment? Then
there was no cost in money or in blocks of time which seemed too
great. Do we now question the worth of the fellowship? Does it
make a real difference to us whether or not it is there for another
person? Do we know that if we are growing Christians then we
are always growing more deeply into the lives of those who com-
pose the Body of Christ?

These are some of the questions which we ask ourselves with
peculiar intensity at this special season of the year. Sometimes one
or two persons, occasionally even three or four, do not recommit.
Often they will renew membership at a later date. Whatever the
difficulty, it is usually first noted at the point of disciplines. Like
the house thermostat which registers heat, our faithfulness in disciplines indicates how well the fire burns in the heart.

These days before recommitment Sunday bring into the open
many repressed reservations and resistances. It is a time of pain and
of healing, a season in which we try with brutal honesty to examine anew our original commitment to Christ.

It is also a time which has a God-given quality, for throughout
the week our members come to the chapel and after an hour of
prayer and adoration, kneel and inscribe their names on the membership roll once again, thanking God that He has provided for us
a people to walk with down all the years. "Once you were no people but now you are God's people" (1 Pet. 2:10).

3 No Abiding Place

And Jesus said to him, "Foxes have holes, and birds of the air have nests; but the Son of man has nowhere to lay his head."

Matthew 8:20

It is difficult to grasp the unchanging aspects of a changing church. We have come increasingly to believe that if the kind of redemptive creative community we envision is to exist, it needs at its heart those who have a lifetime commitment not only to Christ but to a particular segment of His people. The dangers that beset us in this hour, we could not have guessed in the beginning.

We still thought then that two would win two and that in twenty-five years the world would be converted and the kingdom of God be established here on earth. We probably would not have stated it quite so naïvely, but in our hearts this is what we believed. It seemed that the Good News would be easy to tell, and who hearing would not respond? Now, fourteen years later, we know that it does not come about in this way. We know a little bit more of what it costs to save another life. We know the years of nurture required to make a mature Christian and we know that the days cry out for this.

We know also the dangers besetting a fellowship that lives deeply into community. We know that the difficulties in relationship which prompted so many of Paul's letters are those of any fellowship where life is being knit to life. A few of us visited Aldersgate Methodist Church in Cleveland, Ohio, when Bob Raines was the minister.* One of the members told us about a person in a study group who had to spend a night in jail before being admitted to a hospital. "Of course," he said, "Bob spent the night with him." We thought about it and said, "Of course he did." This is the way it has to be. Redemption and salvation are more than high-sounding ecclesiastical words when we live them out on the streets and alleys where we dwell.

Along the way come many temptations to turn back. If we do not want to walk out on our commitment to Christ, we would like to walk out on our commitment to the people of Christ. We rationalize that we can keep the vertical relationship while giving up the horizontal. The two are inseparable. One cannot belong to Christ without belonging to His community, or to the community without belonging to Him in whom it coheres.

This means that we do not leave because we have wanderlust or need a change, or because the job opportunities are better in another city, or because the demands become too great, or because things have not turned out as we had hoped. The call to leave this fellowship has to be a call of the Lord confirmed in the heart of this people. As there was once a reception service, there is now a departure service—the farewell of a community to a brother who is called of God to do a work of God in another place. And as we go we have the knowledge that in the next place is a people of God whose life we will enter into.

We have come to know that building up the church of Jesus Christ is the only task which has significance. In it we can find ultimate meaning. We are not looking for that thing which may happen next week, next month, or next year. We believe ourselves to be engaged this very moment in that which is the hope of the world. Our commitment is to the Lord of that redemptive community which has the task of pushing back its boundaries until it holds the world. There will be no peace or healing in our day unless little islands of *koinonia* can spring up everywhere—islands

---

* Rev. Robert A. Raines, now minister of First Methodist Church, Germantown, Penna.

where Christ is, and because He is we can learn to live in a new way.

Against this backdrop of our enduring life in Christ, which is of time and beyond time, there is that part of our life which is forever changing, never static. This is true of any living organism. The pattern of our life in any one year will not necessarily be that of another year. Three years from now a dual, streamlined highway is scheduled to cut through our lovely old building. No one has yet raised the question of looking for another location or of buying property for a future building, though we all know that a highway approaches. On occasion we have wondered aloud where we will be three years hence, but each of us realizes that the other is aware that we cannot plan this far ahead. We do not now know the kind of building which will best hold and deepen and extend our life together at some future time.

This raises another, loosely related question: What would happen to the Church of the Saviour if it lost not its building but its minister? It is asked by those persons who feel that the Church of the Saviour exists as the vital fellowship it is because Gordon Cosby has brought to it unusual gifts of leadership. Our answer is, "We don't know." We have asked ourselves this lonely question and have decided that we would just gather together and pray, and wait for the Holy Spirit to guide us.

Other religious communities have taken precaution to assure their continuance where we have taken none. The Taize community in France, where the brothers make a lifetime commitment to the community, has written into its rule: "The prior appoints an assistant prior to second him and to assure a continuity after him." It seems good that this is done at Taize, but for us it does not seem the way. Could we name now the man whom God would raise up for another hour? Furthermore, while the church of Christ must endure, the institution of the Church of the Saviour as we know it need never put its energy into the preservation of its own life except as dictated by the Holy Spirit.

But perhaps this is to beg the real question, for those who ask it are asking a deeper one: Does an especially endowed person make the difference or is commitment the vital factor? If we could answer, "A gifted person," we would all be at ease, even those of us who enjoy the benefits of gifted leadership, for the Lord does not give the same talents to everyone. But if we answer, "Commitment," it matters little if it be the commitment of a single man or of many; there would be upon our own lives a call and a judgment. And yet who would have the answer other than commitment, for this means that the promise is to all. One lives in this fellowship and becomes aware that Gordon Cosby is a reconciler, a person whom others gravitate toward, one who gives to those he touches a sense of worth and destiny. But the reason for it is commitment. The person who visits with Gordon is aware that here is a man who has a living relationship with God; and deep in one's own soul is the whisper, "You, too, can have this relationship." Gordon Cosby does not walk alone; he walks with a people and he is a product of the fellowship even as that fellowship is a product of him. He knows what each of us knows: The church is not going to be different until someone in it is different.

God waits for each of us to hear Him say, "Behold, I do a new thing—through you!" The question is always: Can we open our lives so that the Holy Spirit may descend and new power break that we may be the kind of person around whom renewal begins?

It is not easy to interpret the structures of the Church of the Saviour because they are the changing part of our life. By structure we mean that framework or group life which provides opportunity for intimate, continuing relationships, enabling us to grow in the life of love and to come to the place where we can effectively stimulate others to love and good works. Not only do we need to be flexible enough to change these structures from time to time, but we must be flexible enough to contain every type of structure—to let our groups be free to find utterly new ways of expression.

In this changing situation, we have discovered what we feel are three valid functions of any structure by which a group effectively measures its life. The first is the nurture of its own members. The group must never forget that one of its primary functions is simply to upbuild its members in love. The second specific function of any group is for it to serve—to come to know itself in the role of the suffering servant. This means that it will exist for sacrificial service. Its third function is to evangelize. The group is not qualified to evangelize until it is willing to serve.

These are the constants against which we have examined our group life and which have accounted for many of the changes we have made over the years.

One of the first structures we experimented with was the fellowship group. The church had from the beginning its School of Christian Living, but after several years it became evident that the primary function of a group—the nurture of its own members —could not be carried out by continual classes. Increase in numerical strength also brought the danger of diminished spirituality. The original nine persons had grown in commitment to one another. Together they had made deep spiritual exploration. They served long hard hours in the renovating of houses and in the making of extra money to meet necessary payments. In addition, at hospitals and in neighborhood projects they had served and evangelized. Everyone was needed and everyone was aware of the point at which he was needed.

Now our number had become thirty and the question was, what would nurture the life of the group at this stage—what conditions were required to continue a vitality reflecting that of the little band of twelve which had centered around Christ? Out of the pondering of this question came the fellowship, or cell groups, as they were sometimes called. The model was the first Christian fellowship; central to the life of each group was prayer, study, and action. All members were urged to read *Alternative to Futility* by Elton Trueblood,* and *Fellowships of Concern* by Harvey Seifert.†

The groups, each composed of no less than four or more than twelve, met on the same night as the School of Christian Living. During the dinner hour and the social period after the classes, the

* New York: Harper & Brothers, 1948.
† Nashville: Abingdon Press, 1949.

members were to watch out for the new explorers of our life in the School of Christian Living, and to be in touch with them in other unstructured situations.

The fellowship groups, like our mission groups now, included Everyman: women and men, single and married, young and old, learned and unlearned, black, white, yellow; those with prison backgrounds; those with country-club rearing; some with sheltered upbringing; some who knew life in all its rawness. They included salesmen, professors, lawyers, teachers, carpenters, housewives, butchers, cabinetmakers. This wide diversity was then and is now one of our richest blessings, but diversity does not become a gift overnight. Its benefits are for those who grow in Christ and let Him break down the partition which divides person from person, group from group, community from community. Several fellowship groups did not have the maturity to survive diversity; they dissolved and formed in new combinations. Others grew rapidly, adding to their ranks until the number exceeded twelve and they divided, although it was hard to leave those with whom they had found intimate spiritual belonging.

For most of us these were adventurous months of learning and growing. We memorized the Letter of Paul to the Ephesians and discovered what it meant to live with Scripture and to have our minds saturated with it. Many experienced a new awakening to Christ. But although we maintained strong programs of study and prayer, no group did anything significant in the way of service. We maintained the building: we continued to do our own carpentry and painting and other homely tasks, but we never came to grips with a service program outside the church. We yearned for it, but something always stood in the way. We had thought that the Holy Spirit would be so focused in these groups that the power developed would be far greater than eight or twelve working separately could have, but that power to witness did not come.

We had been aware that if we concentrated on a program of service we would be in danger of becoming a group concerned with social issues only, rather than being the church at the point of concern—a people living a life together so that the *koinonia* existed for others to experience. We were also aware that in order not to conform to the world the tendency would be to withdraw from it. The fellowship groups with their theoretical emphasis on prayer and service seemed to present an answer that would keep the inward and the outward movement in balance. But in practice it never worked out. With our various gifts and time schedules and calls, it was natural that we would have difficulty finding an outreach to which everyone within the group could respond. We failed to understand this at the time and we blamed ourselves, thinking that if we were more in Christ the unifying action of the Holy Spirit would give us a common mind at this point of mission. We were seeking conformity when we belonged to a God who thought up individuality. We were to know this later; at the time we could only begin to guess that the fellowship groups were preparation for something else not then known to us. Step by step we were to move toward it.

The day came when we cut off the groups from the School of Christian Living. It was in the year following the publication in both the *Christian Herald* and *Reader's Digest* of an article by Catherine Marshall.* That article told the story of some persons who had come to our church and had their lives changed. It stirred hope in the hearts of many who read it, which is what should happen when one tells the story of a church. From all over the country came letters and telephone calls—and then there were people who just came, who gathered up children and belongings and traveled long distances with the conviction that the Lord God had pointed out to them a new country.

We had always prayed that God would use us despite our limitations, and we were staggered by His answer. We were busy in that year. Members spent long hours answering letters and visiting with new friends. Our times together were always occasions of ministering to the strangers in our midst, many of whom are now our most able ministers. With the passing months members began

---

* "Human Nature Can Be Changed," *Christian Herald*, Dec. 1953; "What I Learned at Gordon Cosby's Church," *Reader's Digest*, Dec. 1953.

to feel a need to be together for corporate prayer and study, and when the fall program was planned it was decided to have the fellowship groups meet on a night separate from class nights so that we could be together as a family of faith. A small nucleus of members would also attend sessions of the School of Christian Living, being held at another time.

For the first weeks this seemed like an ideal structure. The members had had a genuine need to be with one another in a corporate time of prayer and study, and there was a deepening of the life of the group. But as the months slipped by and the demands upon us grew less, something happened in the group that was like the going out of a light. Always when we met, it had been as a great pageant, only "pageant" did not describe it. It was a supernatural community that met—a community whose total was more than the sum of its parts. Have you ever been with a group of people and guessed that they must be very extraordinary people because of their excitement and wonder? And then have you considered that group person by person and found that each was very ordinary, though very beautiful: one a clerk, another a bricklayer; then you remembered that one was a fisherman and one was a tax collector, and another—He was the Son of God.

The Christian community knows this. That which makes it more than it is, is the gift of the Holy Spirit. This is the breath which blows upon the fellowship gathered. When that wind ceased to blow across our times together, we came to a pass which was bewildering. We limped through the weeks. If there was any aliveness in the group it was because of those who were also coming on the night the School of Christian Living met. Here was the answer: Over 75 per cent of our members had cut themselves off from the church's main arm of evangelism, the school. We had ceased to be the Christian Church when we were no longer seeking to give our lives away.

We did then what we shall do again when we do not know what the pattern of tomorrow should be. Each member committed himself to pray daily for the next step of the church. We shared our thoughts whenever we talked and once a week gathered in our chapel for an hour of silent prayer. After the hour anyone could share with the larger group his creative thinking or any insights that had come. Out of this period of six weeks came a totally new structure.

We divided our membership of about sixty persons into four groups, meeting once a week on Monday, Tuesday, Wednesday, and Friday. Each group was responsible for the nonmembers who came on its night. Each group had its minister or moderator; a counselor, who would be available for conferences; a worship leader, who was in charge of the worship period and in a real sense responsible for the group's growth in awareness of God and of oneness as a group; a co-ordinator of the prayer vigil, who arranged for those in the group to join the vigil of prayer made up of people who agreed to spend one hour each month in the chapel, praying for the needs of the church and its people. There was also a work director, a fel-lowship leader, a building steward, a registrar to keep the school records, and other personnel which were needed to make for a smooth and ordered night. Some of the less demanding assignments were filled by new participants in the school. In one sense each of the nights was a church in itself.

This plan placed on each person a larger share of the responsi-bility for the whole of the family life within the total church, which is the opposite from the practice of centralizing the church's life in the staff and in committees, with the result that the people know very little of the life of the church. The mission of the church was back on all of us so that we knew the inner movements of life as well as all those places where the church was reaching out.

Our four nights eventually became consolidated into three, and existed in this pattern for many months. We would have continued indefinitely in this structure, but as in the fellowship groups, we still faced the question of outreach. From the very beginning, mis-sion had been central to the life of our church, as we feel it is central to Christianity. Day in and day out we were working faith-fully with despairing people. We had watched Christ capture new areas of their lives and make them ministers unto us who had been

ministers unto them. At many places our people were engaged in
service projects at great cost to themselves. But we still did not
have those structures which enabled us to penetrate into deep
places of the city's life, to be spiritual commando forces for the
kingdom of God. We had talked about being hard-hitting task
forces moving into the world of business and art and drama and
music and industry and international relations, and we were in
these worlds as individuals witnessing to Christ so that people
we worked with and talked with and played with knew that Christ
was Lord with us, but no place was there the strong corporate witness of the people of God.

It was disappointing to many of us. By this time, we had hoped,
we would be working in the slums of the city: rebuilding a house
perhaps, claiming a block for Christ to whom it belonged; some
thought that perhaps God could speak to government through His
church; others were concerned with the care of the emotionally
ill and wanted the church to be able to say something definite to
the country concerning the care of these sick. We were vague about
what to do, but those of us who had definite concerns began to
wonder if we could ever do anything unless we could be with
others who had similar concerns. From that point it was not difficult to begin to think in terms of organizing our groups on the
basis of specific missions.

Strangely enough we did not easily make this transition to mission groups. We have those special times when we seem to be in the
spirit and make large decisions with great ease, and then we have
those times when we know ourselves to be a prayerless, disobedient,
stiff-necked people.

It was our nonmembers who had a difficult time understanding
the framework of four nights. At the point of the mission groups
it was the members who appeared confused. While the majority
wanted it, some reacted as though the whole idea of mission were
new. In one way it was new. Our thinking was sharpened and
focused and more definite. We had talked about going into the
depressed areas of our city, but it was possible now that a structure would be provided which would enable a person to say yes or

no to the project. Whenever we can be definite, we get to know
ourselves better.

In the spring of 1958 before Gordon and Mary went to Switzerland to be at the Ecumenical Institute of the World Council of
Churches for several weeks, Gordon preached a sermon in which
he attempted to interpret again what some of us meant by mission
groups. He said:

The whole concept of mission is not as difficult as we have wanted to
believe. It is difficult to get hold of with our minds, because it involves
us at the point of response, and whenever we get involved at this point of
discipleship—of cost—then we have a stake in not understanding it.

What is meant by a mission group? The Church is a people which is
sharing in the mission of Jesus Christ. This is what is meant by the
Church. As I discover what aspect of that mission is mine, and as you
discover your mission, and they happen to coincide, then we become part
of a mission group. It is that simple. If God calls me at the point of
international relations and he calls you at this point, and we need one
another to work together, we are a combination of persons on mission
within a mission group.

Who cares what form it takes? Who knows what the details of it will
be, when it meets and how it goes about its task? This is not important.
The important thing is that this group discover the guidance of God step
by step, and be so attuned to His will, and so flexible that it shall be able
to discover what He has in mind.

This is all you mean by a mission group: Two or more persons who
have been grasped by the same concept of God's task for them, and who
have been grasped by God, which is deeper and more profound than being
grasped by a concept.

Throughout the summer that Mary and Gordon were away, we
talked and argued about mission groups. They were to be the same
as our fellowship groups except that the members would be on mission at a certain point of need and adopt the disciplines necessary to
accomplish that mission—disciplines additional to those of prayer
and study. Some were fired by the idea of at last getting into in-
tensive service; others continued to look blank whenever the idea
was mentioned; and still others were openly hostile. When we

planned our fall program that year, it held every kind of structure because we found ourselves as a membership at different places. The School of Christian Living was again scheduled for one night a week. Those who wanted to continue in fellowship groups met on this night so they could be a part of this evangelizing arm of the church. The third and new structure was the mission groups, which had from two to fifteen persons. A new class in vocation was also added. It was a seminar-type class with a discipline in prayer. The object was to help each participant discover his own special vocation—that place where God would have him on mission. Class members dealt specifically with the question: "What does God have for me to do?" It was in one of these vocation classes that the idea of our coffee house first caught hold.

The vocation class helped with the transition to our present mission-group plan. New people coming into the church now do not have to grapple with the issue of mission in the same way. They often touch the church first at the point of one of its mission groups, and asking how they can be a part of one of these groups, learn about the School of Christian Living. Even those who start in the School of Christian Living are easily instructed in the meaning of mission, for we have simply to say, "Come and see."

There are a number of mission groups which minister to the internal life of our congregation in order that it may be strong to do its work as it moves out into the city. There is the library group, which makes the purchases for our library and keeps us informed and stimulated on new books. There is the teachers' mission group, whose purpose is to shape a program for our children as deeply meaningful as that which their parents know in the School of Christian Living. There is the retreat mission, which is instructing us in retreat in order that our lives may grow more deeply into the life of God, and the Dayspring group, which is giving guidance and direction to all that is happening on our 175 acres in the Maryland countryside.

There are several ways in which we move out into the city to penetrate its life and "fill the breach between the peace of God and the hunger of men." One is the Rockville House Congregation. In

this congregation we try to live out part of our life in a neighborhood and seek to serve that neighborhood. Another way is a coffee
house, which we call the Potter's House. Here we try to be in the
market place, as it were, hoping that as we can be a people in whom
the Holy Spirit dwells others will enter into the gospel. Still another way is an art center—the Potter's House Workshop—through
which we are seeking to bring a little part of the world of art under
the Lordship of Christ. Now we plan to move into the depressed
areas of our city. Even if we touch no more than a tiny segment of
the need, we want for our own soul's sake to be with the poor. Another unfolding way is a Renewal Center, where we can gather a
few of the sick of our city and give to them the best medical care
and counseling help we are able to provide, and the prayers of our
people.

All the missions are flexibly conceived and may change any
time on the basis of new experience or obedience to God's leading.
There are groups being dreamed of as this is written, and in a few
months they may be in existence. There also have been a few
groups that started and petered out before moving into a specific
area of concern. And there were those which came into existence
for a particular task and having accomplished that task were dissolved. One such group was the marriage group, which had crucial,
dramatic months together and which changed the participants
forever. The mission of the group was to evaluate material on the
subject of marriage which might be useful in a course or in counseling. The group began with evaluating materials and ended by
evaluating their marriages. They discovered that although the
material on the subject was immense, too little of it was written
from the viewpoint of committed Christians. They asked, "Does
Jesus Christ make any difference in a marriage?" and then they
searched themselves for the answer. One member said, "We looked
deep into our own marriages and related to the group things that
no partner had told the other. We stirred up old wounds and our
marriages at one time or another were all in crisis. But today I
have a better marriage because we worked out what we felt to be
the essence of a marriage. You can't have a marriage if you can't

talk about what is deep on your heart, which means the other person has to be willing to listen." In their weeks together the members of this group wrote the first draft of a book, with chapters on communication, sex, community, love, money, divorce, vision.

The mission structure helped us to fulfill what we had defined as the three functions of any group: (1) to nurture its own members, (2) to serve, and (3) to evangelize. We are often asked if the fellowship group, with its emphasis on prayer and study, is not necessary preparation for participation in a mission group. Our answer is that fellowship groups were necessary for us because we knew no other way, but we now permit a person to be on mission with us after two classes in the School of Christian Living if he continues to take the classes. Within the mission groups nonmembers have been caught up in prayer and study as well as service, in a way that is not possible even in a fellowship group. It is the laboratory situation for much that we talk about in our classes.

We can speak of the hardships of changing structures because we have lived through them. We know how difficult it is and always will be, but we know also that one of the reasons our church has its relative power is because it has been willing to make changes, with all that this involves.

Sometimes it has been bewildering to nonmembers. Some have asked as we pondered a new step, "Is the Church of the Saviour to be dissolved?" While others have inquired, "Is it too late to become a member of the Church of the Saviour?"

Their questions have given us an opportunity to interpret our church at the point of a person's asking. We explained that our structures would never be static, and that the experiences we were having today would enable us to do the next thing, and that what we were doing now would probably be quite different from what we would be doing three or five or ten years from now. We never have expected to hit upon that final stable structure. This is important for a church to understand, for when it starts to be the church it will constantly be adventuring out into places where there are no tried and tested ways. If the church in our day has few

prophetic voices to sound above the noises of the street, perhaps
in large part it is because the pioneering spirit has become foreign
to it. It shows little willingness to explore new ways. Where it does
it has often been called an experiment. We would say that the
church of Christ is never an experiment, but wherever that church
is true to its mission it will be experimenting, pioneering, blazing
new paths, seeking how to speak the reconciling Word of God to its
own age.

It cannot do this if it is held captive by the structures of another
day or is slave to its own structures. This is not easy to grasp. It is
not a concept that we lay hold of once and then have forever. It is
easy for one generation to overthrow the structures of another and
to think itself bold and adventurous. But the test comes in whether
we can part with the structure we ourselves have created, for new
forms, like the old, can come to represent safeness and security. The
young have not proved more pioneering than those who have gone
before them until they have been tested. Strangely enough, we
often find that those who protest change the most are those who
were most attracted by the adventurousness of the group.

No person or group is forever free from the temptation to settle
down into mediocrity, and we all experience our times of timidity.
It takes courage to walk into the unknown, a willingness to take
upon ourselves the burden of anxiety.

Whatever the fears, they need to be understood by those who
would help usher in the new. We must know that no new form
or structure, no matter how creative it is, seems good to the person
who feels that it will by-pass him. Our security becomes rooted in
Christ, not in structures, when we have a fellowship that helps us
to belong, that cares enough to let us know we are needed, that
prays enough to help us find the peculiar task which only we can
do. In our own church we endured the times of change to discover that the life of a church does not lie in its structures. We
learned with ever changing programs that the organization and
institutional forms are important only because the life they hold
is important. That life is unpredictable, breaking out anew in un-

expected places and in unexpected ways. The structures are to hold it as wineskins are to hold wine. As new life breaks in upon us, new structures are needed.

We had times when the decision to move on loomed so large that it was difficult to bring ourselves to face all that it entailed. There is always a transitional phase in which nothing seems settled. You can live into that time with your imagination and catch anticipatory anxiety, a congregation all stirred up and milling around, and you ask yourself, "What if this should prove wrong? What if after changing the way of a people there is the discovery that the new is not nurturing the life of the community as it should, or storming the strongholds of evil as was hoped?" These are the waves from a cautious past that wash over us at times. The important thing is that they not leave us drifting as though the church had no Saviour.

Change can, of course, be an escape. Those of us who have too restless spirits need to be certain that we do not seek in changing patterns evasion of the challenges and pressures in the present situation. When we part too easily with that which we have known, perhaps we have not loved well enough.

But those of us who err on the other side need to be reminded that change is one of the characteristics of the Christian community. It should be so much the order of the day that the long, undisturbed stretches would make us wonder. We belong to a revolutionary movement. Our task is world-wide. We have listened in on the sorrow of God for the lonely and the beaten, for the confused and the driven, for the homeless and the despairing, and we have arrayed ourselves against the principalities of evil. Wherever greed, and lust, and quest for power, and prejudice, and privilege exist, they should find in the Christian Church a threat and an army on the move with a strategy that will change with the shifting lines of the enemy.

4 Dayspring

. . . the dayspring from on high hath visited us, to give light to them that sit in darkness and in the shadow of death, to guide our feet into the way of peace.

LUKE 1:78-79, AV

Dayspring might be described as 175 acres of land in the rolling hill-country of Maryland. We make attempts to be objective about many phases of our church's life, knowing full well that we do not wholly succeed. But when it comes to Dayspring, we do not even try.

We love all her ways: the woods, the fields, the trails, quiet spots and spacious stretches, the lessons we have learned there, the still-born dreams we have had for this place as well as those that have found root in her soil. We even find the seasons different here, for summer and winter and spring and fall touch this land in a lavish, spendthrift way, or so it seems to those of us who grew up in cities of concrete.

Have you ever watched a man pause to look at the property he owns and noted that something happens between him and the land he calls "my land?" It yields to him its secret and he yields to it his secret and one knows that they are mysteriously bound. We are like that about Dayspring. It has made contemplatives of us all, even those who take a dim view of the mystical life.

Dayspring was first mentioned in the spring of 1952—that is, the idea of a place such as Dayspring. Someone said it would be nice to have a place in the country where we could go for days of retreat. It was just a thought, one of those wonderful thoughts that it never hurts to have and that fantasy can build on, but it had to stay in the realm of fantasy.

We had moved from our building on 19th Street just two years before. With thirty-five members and a participating fellowship of one hundred we had obligated ourselves to purchase and maintain our present building, which represented an investment of $90,000. There was no wealthy person in our congregation and hardly any who were financially comfortable. A house in the country was not in the realm of possibilities, but the unthinkable somehow seemed very thinkable to a few of us. By the summer of 1952 that far-fetched thought had caught in the hearts of our people.

In the fall of 1952 the Council of the church appointed three young women to look for a place. They were sent out with difficult instructions: They must find a farm large enough for a general fellowship area; it must have a spot which could be developed as a retreat area; it must have a site appropriate for a children's camp; it must have an area suitable for farming, to help cut down the overhead through the years. Furthermore, the terrain must be such that each area would be separate and at a distance from the others. It must be within an hour's drive from the church. It must be easy to locate. In order that it might be used right away it must have a farmhouse on it in reasonably good condition. Most difficult of all, it must be purchasable for less than $40,000, with favorable terms of financing! Even so, we did not have the money on hand for the down payment, should such a place be found.

Throughout the fall and winter Carolyn Johnson, Jessie Henderson, and Sally Jumper searched. A few weeks before Easter we had that certain feeling that things were going to happen. Kathryn Campbell prepared a little brochure which put into word pictures that which had been conceived in prayer. She aptly titled it "Treasure in a Field." We agreed that our Easter offering would go to buy this field when we stumbled on it. Our members were already tithing and had given all possible reserves for the purchase of our church building. Some of our people took extra jobs, others went without legitimate expenditures, and many arranged for loans which could be paid back over a one- or two-year period. Dayspring, like every other dream that has unfolded in this fellowship, was built on the sacrificial offerings of money, energy, time, and prayer.

On Easter Sunday, 1953, with a charged expectancy in the air, we came to church. George Selden, who was to preside over our festival barbecues at Dayspring, helped count the special offering that Sunday; it was slightly more than $9,000. We were now ready to act when the right place was found.

In May we found that place. Our committee had looked at fifty farms. The last real estate office they visited called Gordon Cosby and said, "We have three girls here, who have indicated that your church is in the market for a farm. If you will send a responsible person, we will be glad to talk to him and show you what we have." Gordon told the gentleman that we had no one more responsible than those three girls and that if he would like to deal with us he would have to deal with them.

They looked at three farms that day. The third was on the road to Damascus—a sign, had they been seeking one. It was approached from a tree-lined dirt road. When it came into view there was a long, panoramic sweep that included a house in reasonably good condition, barns, pasture land, woods, and a stream that could be dammed to make a pond. Each of us who went out to look at it knew with a certainty that it belonged to us and we belonged to it. The members agreed unanimously on the purchase. Only one question was raised: Was it large enough to let the dreams we had for it unfold? Each of us had his own dream—a retreat center, a children's home, a radio-TV station, an amphitheater, an old people's home, a fellowship lodge. All of these, along with many others, had been seriously considered. But one binding, unifying vision held them together: It was to be a place where the lives of everybody who touched it could become more deeply rooted in the life of God. Here wounds would be exposed and healed by Christ's love, here we would work and pray and play together, here the loved and the unloved would be equally welcome.

Everyone who wanted an area of responsibility could find it at Dayspring. There would be work to do for many years to come. One of the first tasks that seemed so unending was picking stones from the fields so the ground could be seeded and cut. At least fifty of us labored on Saturdays for a month, piling those stones to be carted away. During the week new stones would work their way out of the ground, or so it seemed. Dozens of other jobs were performed in those first months. The farmhouse was repaired and painted inside and out; the barns were put into condition; a pit was dug for a pond, and one day the water flowed into it. Later we stocked it with fish. The vineyards and orchard were carefully planted, pruned, and tended, and to our amazement yielded fruit. Dogs and cats and a saddle horse were our first animals. Later, to the delight of the children, two burros came to live in the stable.

The first major section which we agreed to develop was the retreat area. By spring of 1954, a year after the purchase of Dayspring, the plans for a retreat lodge had been drawn, permits granted, and the footings dug. The gifts of our people made possible the purchase of material as it was needed, and the Saturday labor of the same people built a lodge where as many as twenty persons could in a time set apart find a deeper friendship with Him who is the Author of life.

The lodge includes a kitchen, a dining room that seats twenty, and a large worship room with a fireplace and bookshelves. One wall is of glass, which lets retreatants look into an untouched wood. The front windows give a view of meadowland which has been used for grazing cattle in one year and for wheatfields and corn in other years. The comfortable chairs are upholstered in the colors of earth: green and gold and brown. There is one picture of Christ in the room, the work of a Jewish artist who visited us and later sent the picture with the explanation, "I wanted you to have a picture of the Christ I met at Dayspring."

Before the lodge was begun we gathered to dedicate the land on which it was to be built and ourselves to the task of its building. Two years later, when it was completed, we met again on the same spot. Elizabeth-Anne Campagna wrote the dedication service, which began with our congregation seated in silence on the ground outside the Lodge of the Carpenter, as we had named it.

Our Father, help us feel thy presence, for otherwise our being here is nothing. We must seek Thee with our whole selves now. This is Thy moment. Help us that it be not lost to us. Here is the work of our hands. Take it for Thy use. We would see Thy glory as it enfolds this house and makes of it a House of God.

Lord, help us clearly to read God's blueprint for our lives. When radiant hopes and dreams are no longer a part of our vision, remake us in this spot, O Lord. May the silence of these woods and good fields hush the clamant voices of our sin. Work Thou a work in our souls, Creator, mighty and complete.

This call to worship was given by Hans Spencer, who for two years had spent every Saturday hammering, instructing, and imparting to us all a love of the task of building. Hans then sounded his hammer twelve times, symbolic of the call of the Apostles, and spoke the words:

> Unless the Lord builds the house,
> those who build it labor in vain.

After a hymn came the litany:

First Carpenter: With our voices we have broken the silence of this tangled thicket. With our tools we have broken the forest floor.

The People: Builder of Life Divine, accept our reverent praise.

First Carpenter: With a good will and comradeship we raised this lodge to Thy honor. Its foundations are firm, its beams are stout, the chimney draws, the windows are frames for Your hills and fields.

The People: Carpenter of Nazareth, inspect this work and use it for Thy glory.

Second Carpenter: We bid Thee come—Nay—Thou hast been here from the first. To draw with us the plans, to lift with us the planks, place the mortar, hang the doors. We could almost hear the sound of Your plane, the ring of Your hammer, the laughter in Your voice—in this, Thy lodging place.

The litany was followed by a reading of Psalm 122, after which another of our carpenters came forward and said:

Solomon built a temple before us, and we would pray, using his words: "But will God indeed dwell on the earth? Behold, heaven and all the earth cannot contain Thee: how much less this house which I have built! Yet listen to this prayer of supplication which we make to Thee this day. . . . that Thine eyes may be open day and night to this place. When we pray, hear Thou in heaven, Thy dwelling place, and when Thou hearest, forgive."

Then came the presentation of the symbols.

The Bible. "This house is to be a place for the study of God's Word."
The *Prie-dieu*. "This house is to be a place of prayer."
The Fire for the Hearth. "This house is to be a place of holy fellowship."
A Green Plant. "This house is to be a place of spiritual growth under God."
The Bread and the Wine. "This house is to be the dwelling place of the Holy Spirit."

After each symbol was presented it was taken into the house and George Markley, whose love and devotion and skill are part of that house, offered the prayer of dedication. Worshipers were then invited to take communion in the dining room.

In silence we left the lodge and the retreat area, which had also been dedicated. Since that time, whenever we have passed through the gate into this area, we have been conscious that it is land set aside for an especial use. No matter what activity may be taking place elsewhere on the farm, here in this portion of it solitude and silence can be found. Here a person's aloneness with God is respected and protected.

On the day of dedication we began our instruction in the nature of retreat. The Lodge of the Carpenter has never been used for planning conferences. Some of our teachers in those days were John Casteel, through his writings, and Douglas Steere, through his book *Time to Spare.** John Casteel later led a retreat for our

---

* Douglas V. Steere (New York: Harper & Brothers, 1949).

potential retreat leaders and Douglas Steere came to help us plan at a crucial point in our development of the retreat area.

Since that June of 1956 we have made many retreats at Dayspring. Nearly every one of our groups has its time of retreat once or twice a year, and there are many of us who slip away to spend a day of quiet at the lodge. Here we have wrestled not only with our problems but, as Jacob did, with the angel, until we knew that we were blessed. We are each of us deeply convinced that we would be living closer to the real center of life if we could take one day a month at Dayspring, but thus far only a small remnant has disciplined its time well enough to follow what we would so ardently recommend.

In addition to our own groups, forty-nine churches in the Washington area used the Lodge of the Carpenter last year. This gives us a special kind of joy, for if ever a church has been nurtured by the larger Christian fellowship, it is this one.

Although the building of the Lodge of the Carpenter was the most celebrated activity at Dayspring over a two-year period, the majority of Saturday workers were engaged in other places at the farm. We repaired fences; limed and fertilized the fields; began our first farming operation; planted hundreds of trees in Arbor Day ceremonies, for at Dayspring there has always been a ceremony for everything, a time when corporately we placed our dreams and our work and the land itself in the hands of God. A bulldozer helped with the work of creating an athletic field, roads through the woods, and the children's play area. Always we found time in the course of the day to approve the progress at the lodge and to be on hand for such important occasions as the laying of the first brick. No phase of this work went unexamined.

Various areas of Dayspring were developed as the members felt that they could carry the responsibility and were willing to give leadership. Our farmers started almost from scratch, without previous knowledge or experience, but there were books to read, and the United States government offers many helps to farmers even when they are not professional.

Our first crop, twenty acres of wheat in the field below the lodge, gave us a profit of $400. But more than that, we came to know each other in a different way as we pitched in on the work when we were needed. Some of us found God in worship days at Dayspring, but others found Him as we worked together in the heat of a blazing sun. I think we all knew in a deep, deep way that life was good on two Saturdays when men and women and children helped, in the sweltering heat, with our first hay crop. One thousand bales were tossed onto our hay wagon and unloaded in the barn.

Our farmers have more recently turned their hands to other things, such as a land-turf operation, landscaping, and a nursery. In the late summer days we gather the grapes and make the communion wine.

Dayspring, like everything else of significance that has been attempted by our church, has taught us two lessons: One, that nothing which is worth doing is ever done without great sacrifice, and two, that every dream in its unfolding has difficult times, times when those who work with it are discouraged, when it seems as though those who were committed to it have lost the vision. Dayspring has known those days. A project would be started, but somehow it would never be completed. Perhaps it was the project of a task-minded person or of a perfectionist who just could not deal with the human situation, for at Dayspring we are up against the carelessness and inexperience of others. Or perhaps we make the discovery that we know very little about work and that we belong to a fellowship that likewise knows little about work. One of our people explained it in terms of grace and law.

At Dayspring we have to be aware that living under Grace requires that we furnish our own discipline in weeding the garden, spraying the vineyard, caring for the golf green, building a fence, painting the barn, or cleaning the Lodge of the Carpenter. No one will tell us that we must do it; no one will fuss when we don't carry through on our elected responsibility; and quite often there will be no one to help us. We are *on our own*. This freedom gets us down. We are accustomed to working by the clock and being paid a salary. We do what we are told and we are told how to do it. We are at a loss when we have to use our own origi-

nality, our ingenuity, and perhaps bring our own materials to work with.
. . . Furthermore, if no one notices what we have done and that we have
gotten a sunburn and splinters in the process, we feel forlorn.

And so Dayspring, like everything else, gave us some hard facts
about ourselves, gave us lessons that we were slow to learn. These
were the valleys without which there could be no mountaintops.

The mountaintop days were many, and in the spring of 1957 we
began to talk about a festival of faith, a time to "sing unto the
Lord a new song." When we began to look into the history of
festivals, we found that in thinking of a festival we walked in
the company of Abraham, of Isaac, of Jacob, of Joseph, of Jesus,
and of Paul, and indeed in the company of all believers.

The one known biographical note on the boyhood of Jesus
records His being at the annual festival of his people. "When
he was twelve years old, they went up according to custom" to the
festival of the Passover. The boy Jesus had grown up knowing
that one of the joys of life was to be with the fellowship gathered.
Although in a sense it is a festival whenever believers come together, there are always special times. Later it cost Jesus His life
to go to such a festival. His friends stood in the Temple, saying,
"What do you think? That he will not come to the feast?"

Paul too had known the importance of a festival of faith. "And
he came to Ephesus and left them there, but he himself entered
into the synagogue and reasoned with the Jews. When they desired
him to tarry a long time with them he consented not. But bade
them farewell, saying, I must by all means keep this feast that
cometh in Jerusalem, but I will return again unto you if God will"
(Acts 18:19-21, AV).

In the tradition of our fathers we began to plan a two-day
festival. Part of the preparation was the building of an amphitheater at Dayspring. On Memorial Day, 1957, we gathered on a
wooded hillside for a simple ground-breaking ceremony. The first
shovelful of dirt was passed from person to person and each one
took a handful, symbolic of his or her share in the work that was
about to begin.

The morning was spent in felling trees and clearing away brush. By noon every tree marked to come down lay on the ground, and there was the sound of axes and saws as they were cut up and moved to a pile to be stacked and burned. In the next weeks our men dug the foundations and poured the footings, and bit by bit the stage was built. It was a beautiful stage, but from a distance it seemed to be crooked! The brick wall, which followed the contour of the ground, just did not match the stage floor, which had been constructed with a level. We could do nothing about it, so we overlooked it as best we could and went on with the work of digging footings for the redwood planks that were to be our benches. As the festival date drew near, we began to work at night by the stage lights. All through the month of August there were informal suppers, several hours of work, and then devotions by the light of a dying fire.

When the day came, not only the amphitheater, but the whole of Dayspring stood in readiness. All the shrubbery had been carefully tended, the barns newly whitewashed, fences painted, lawns and fields freshly cut, and even the crooked stage was no longer crooked. In the summer of 1956 Ian Cramb, who was the chief stonemason at the Iona Community in Scotland, had visited Dayspring for a few weeks, and during his visit he built a stone bridge across the brook. Tom Hubers had watched Ian build the bridge, and a few days before the festival, sitting alone on an amphitheater bench, he looked at the stage and decided that the error could be hidden from sight by a row of stones atop the wall. A trowel, a bag of cement, and stones collected from the woods were the only materials he needed. Stonemasonry was new to Tom, but the work, like the thought, was inspired. He placed jagged stones along the whole length of the wall and there at the center, correcting our error, the cross.

That first festival of faith had everything: music, sermons, drama, pageantry. It began with David Longfellow summoning us to worship with the blowing of a trumpet. We knew then why it was that C. S. Lewis had his character Screwtape say that what he missed most of all, in his alienation from heaven, was the sound of trumpets in the morning.

After worship, there were workshops in choreography, painting, crafts, prayer, drama, foreign relations, and music. All of them had the theme, "We Would See Jesus." These particular workshops were chosen because they were the areas in which we had gifted leaders. At one o'clock a "loaves-and-fishes" box luncheon was served. Dr. J. P. Allen of Alexandria, Virginia, and Dr. Norman V. Hope of Princeton Theological Seminary preached the two festival sermons that day. When evening fell, tall torches lit the trails to the amphitheater. The play, presented on the two evenings, was James Bridie's *Tobias and the Angel*, which meant that each festival day ended with the angel Raphael throwing off his robe and striding up the woodland hill of our amphitheater to disappear in the darkness. It was easy for us to believe in angels, for the spirit of Christ dwelt among us, full of grace and truth.

We have had other festivals of faith since then, and will have them down the years. We shall have them in order that there may continue to be, as Holy Scripture says, a time of remembering: "And thou shalt remember that thou wast a bondman in the land of Egypt" (Deut. 15:15, AV). Not only shall we remember our history as the people of God, but the history of our own brief days back to that time when we were strangers to the covenant of promise, "having no hope and without God in the world." Our festivals shall be, therefore, a time of thanksgiving for our deliverance out of bondage and of renewed commitment to Him in whom we have our freedom.

Our festivals shall also be a time when we introduce our children to the faith in the way in which Jesus was introduced. Hopefully, when the feast is over we shall find them as Jesus was found, "sitting among the teachers, listening to them and asking them questions."

Our festivals shall be not only a time when we celebrate what is ours and help children to find it, but a time when we can introduce strangers to our faith. Perhaps in the pageantry of a festival a child's spirit and a man's spirit are made ready to listen and to ask.

Another summer activity at Dayspring is camping. The campsite is located in the dense woodland area beyond the orchard and ball field. Here we have had ecumenical camps for collegians, junior high camps, family camps, and camps for children from the depressed areas of our city. Though the structure of each camp varies with age group and gathering, the purpose is the same: to live life together.

The periods of camping give us long, quiet hours to be with each other apart from the usual routine of our days. Somehow they are always days marked by a newness—perhaps because we are free from the usual responsibilities of home and office, or it may be because when a worship service is over or a piece of work completed we do not have to get up and go some place. We are free for a time to be together. We may be worn out from unaccustomed hours of muscle-tiring work, but we are not tired in our separate little dwellings. We share our tiredness around campfires, and often fatigue gives way to talk of how to let a city know that there is a Dayspring.

We talked about sharing our own experience of camping, but we could not simply say to certain agencies, "Dayspring is available to you for so many weeks. Gather together some of the people you are working with and have a camp." There would have to be a little core of people who knew the Giver of the common life. We were committed to the way of Jesus who invited a person here and a person there until the number was twelve. When we have a camp for under-privileged children, we have one counselor to every two children in order that they may know the healing love of God which comes through a relationship.

From the beginning, overnight retreat lodgings were a part of the dream of Dayspring, but the fullness of time for it was the summer of 1961. Our mission groups had placed us in the world. We could not possibly do what we saw to do. Somehow we knew as a fellowship that our mission as the church in the world would be in peril if this outward movement did not have a corresponding movement of retreat.

It was a summer when we were confronted with the questions of commitment at a new and deeper level. Many things stood between us and this next step; one of them was abundance. Could we give God our abundance as a fellowship in the way that once we had given him our poverty? We now had properties to attend to, estates to administer. All that we had done, God had touched. The farm that three girls had purchased for us at the sum of $36,000 was appraised at $280,000. We had opened a coffee house and the world was at its doors. But more than that, the church in many places was asking for prayers and guidance, and in increasing numbers visitors were coming to touch that which seemed to hold hope.

Somehow, without our being wholly aware of it, our light had been set on a hill. The result was that there was more work than one fellowship of seventy members could do. We had the task of ministering to the larger Christian fellowship, to our periphery group here of 130 people who were exploring with us the Christian life, and beyond this, scores of strangers to the Christian way that our mission groups had put us in contact with. All this crowded in on us while we tried to remain true to those covenant relationships of the families in which we had been set and to that covenant we had with one another as the family of faith. The question was, were we going to stick with it and work it through, or here and there were we going to pull back and let go the footholds we had in alien territory? The things we needed to learn if we were to continue were many.

We needed to learn to live from a quiet center. We needed to learn the attitude of leisure when there was no leisure. We needed to learn how to let a friend know that we cared when we were pressured by the weight of unfinished work. We needed to learn to give a task wholly to God. And we needed to learn to forgive one another not only petty hurts but wounds that had gone deep. The level of commitment at which we stood had made us vulnerable, and being vulnerable, we had hurt one another. We had been up against each other in thoughtless, inconsiderate, irresponsible, uncaring moments. Could we call each person "friend"—those who were or who would be the enemies of our peace? Could we stay with it over the long haul when the sheen of newness was gone? Could we keep expectancy for a human life against all logic and reason because we leaned unto Him with whom all things were possible, or were we going to give our sick and distraught over to "proper agencies," to go professional, as the church so often has in our day.

These were a few of the questions that awaited our answer. This was the backdrop against which our people considered whether or not we should have overnight retreats at Dayspring. Did we really believe that the renewal of the church in our day was dependent on prayer? Could we again give sacrificially so that we could take the step that would give us new opportunity to get our lives more deeply grounded in the life of God, learn the lessons that come with abundance and ever unfolding vistas?

A Sunday afternoon was set aside for the dedication of the land on which the lodgings were to be built. We needed $10,000 to begin building; the rest could be borrowed against Dayspring. There was to be no fund-raising campaign that would extend over the months. Our people knew that the issue would be decided in one afternoon. The amount needed was the same as that required eight years before to purchase Dayspring. We prayed. We prayed with expectancy, but some of us just did not know how it was going to be done. When Sunday afternoon came and we looked at the little gathering of 150 men and women and children in our amphitheater, it seemed even less likely. If there had only been some prosperous-looking folk on that hillside; but most of us looked a bit tired, and we knew each other well enough to know that we did not have any money. How long it takes us to know that God chooses the lame and the halt and the blind and the weak to confound the wise. How long it takes to accustom a people to miracles in their midst.

Onto our amphitheater stage walked two of our men, cast by Elizabeth-Anne in the roles that would interpret our thoughts. Their reading ended with the first reader distributing bits of earth from Dayspring to each of us gathered. Then the second reader and the people assembled read responsively.

Second Reader: What token is this that you are receiving? It seems but a clod, a bit of earth. What does it signify?

All the People: We hold in our hands the earth of Dayspring, blessed soil which has long since been dedicated to the God who made it. We seek to know His will for its future use.

Second Reader: What is the cost of so dear a dwelling? A pound of flesh for peace?

All the People: It will cost us more than that. It will cost us moneys from our treasures, and thought from our minds, sweat from our brows, and consecration of our souls.

Second Reader: I've heard it said here, "Thou shalt love the Lord thy God with all thy heart, with all thy soul, with all thy mind." This you profess. Methinks it is the money that troubles you. The prayer places would arise easily if they could be founded on sweet vespers and cemented with joyful fellowship, and nailed with pious sighs, and glassed about with fine visions. He who is Head of the Project may indeed be Spirit, but a Spirit who is at home in His earth, knowing lengths and breadths and cost per square foot. What a God we have—who knew a true plane and a sound roof—who carpentered a thousand beams—and who stands on the top of yon rise surveying His Dayspring, ready for the building of a place of retreat and prayer. I, for one, plan to join Him there.

But first I shall place this bit of Dayspring in this vessel, as a pledge that I shall give Him a gift of money.

You who would join me in this holy building—bring your bit of earth and your gift of money or your true pledge, and place them here.

We placed our gifts of money and pledges in the jug that stood on the amphitheater stage and walked silently up the hill to the retreat area, followed the dirt road to the lodge, and then into the woods to the site of the new building. We left two of our company to count the money and report the totals. By the time the simple dedicatory prayer was over, they had joined us. They announced that the offering totaled $9,800. Two in that gathering increased their pledges and the amount now stood at over $10,000. Under ordinary circumstances, this never could have happened. It was the grace of God which had been shown, for "in a severe test of affliction, their abundance of joy and their extreme poverty have overflowed in a wealth of liberality on their part."

This is the kind of thing that happened in the early church. It was a natural thing. It is unnatural that it does not happen more often in the church of God. Perhaps it requires too much faith, too much even though it be required of only a few and not of all.

The rustling sound of the wind trapped in the trees of Dayspring remind us always that the "winds of God" blow here.

Miracle after miracle has touched its unfolding. Carolyn Johnson (later Mrs. Thomas Hubers), starting out to search for a farm that could be our retreat center, little guessed that she and her future husband would one day be ministers of Dayspring and would build the first house of what we hope will be the Dayspring resident community. Tom Hubers had never heard of the Church of the Saviour then. He was to hear of it on a day of deep despair when his sister placed in his hands a *Reader's Digest* with an article about a church in Washington, D. C. It was easy for Tom to come; he just packed his bag and came.

It was a more difficult move for Ralph and Alice and little Amy Talbot. Ralph had a $25,000-a-year job with Eastman Kodak in Rochester, New York. They had a home and deep roots in their community and to come when they did meant that they gave up half their retirement fund. But, like Tom, they just packed their bags and came. When God orders a man out into a new country, the man does not reply, "But first I must . . ." Ralph and Alice have started a tree nursery at Dayspring. Each morning at nine they take their young daughter to school and head for the farm. Recently we had a retreat for ministers at the Lodge of the Carpenter. One of them looked out the window and saw Ralph Talbot on the tractor, and he said to the others, "I've just been sitting here all afternoon and that man out there on the tractor makes me feel guilty." Little did the minister guess that Ralph Talbot knew what he had yet to learn—how to enter into the rest of God. This is one of the secrets that Dayspring will impart to those who share her life. But it is a secret that does not belong to Dayspring alone. It can be found in the place of your dwelling, for it belongs to the people of God who pray when the sun comes up and when the sun goes down.

5 Kingdom Outposts

The adults of our church are on mission to the children of our church. We are not trying to involve the children in a Sunday school program, hoping that they in turn will involve their parents in the church.

We insist on the participation of at least one parent in the life of the church because we believe the child cannot enter into a faith that is being denied by the people who are most significant to him. Children pick up more from the home atmosphere than from anything they might be told on a Sunday morning at a church school. It is at home that it is made difficult or easy for them to rest back in the grace of God, to believe or disbelieve in love. The home is the outpost of the Christian Church in the world and it is here that the church succeeds or fails, according to the faithfulness of those involved.

The Christian home is the basic functioning unit of a redeemed society. It is unlike any other home because it seeks to do one thing, and that is to embody the love of God and to bring into the orbit of that love every person who touches it.

A child finds this out in many ways, and not the least of them is prayer. Our children learn very young to pray for others. The toddlers in our church school, if they have Jessie Ashton for a teacher, go home on Sunday with the name of a classmate pinned to their coats, so that their parents will know which classmate their child is to pray for during the week. We smile, ourselves, when we meet one of these wee creatures with his prayer responsibility tacked to his garments, but ours is the age that has established the importance of the baby years, and we want deep in their unconscious the knowledge that God is, and that they are members not of an island house but of the household of God whose love covers all homes.

Our parents commit themselves to at least one regular prayer period with their children daily. If you are visiting in one of the homes of our church when it is bedtime for the children, you will probably be invited to participate in family prayers. Even the world of an adult seems more securely in the hands of God when you have knelt beside a bunk bed with a family of children, or been a part of the line-up in front of a couch, or sat in a circle of prayer with the very young. The ways and customs and rituals of families differ, but the language of prayer is that of the spirit, and it is the same from household to household.

Muriel Lipp in describing prayer time with her children said she had found that the best time to pray with them was at bedtime because this was when they most needed assurance and affection and preparation for the night, which holds for a child not only rest, but fear and separation too. She has also found that this is a time when her children are most open and share most easily both the hurts and discoveries of the day.

Muriel prays for her baby silently, as she rocks her. Her five-year-old boy and three-year-old girl like her to sit by them on their beds and extemporize. They feel free to interrupt with their own prayers or to add to hers. She prays with each child individually and tries to keep the time so protected that her children will know that however fractured their relationship has been during the day, this is a time when she listens to them and when they can be sure of her complete attention.

"Our prayers," she says, "often sum up our day. We thank God for specific friends, relatives, things, and experiences. We talk about problems, such as a big boy up the block who said, 'Get out

of my way, little kid!' We confess our faults, and here I shed my
guilt for unfair punishments and grievances I have committed
against them. We pray to be as He wants us to be."

She finds, as most parents do, that in the time of prayer with
her children she is most fully aware that her chief responsibility is
to cherish them as the persons God made them and to point them
toward Him for their fulfillment.

One of the specific ways the church helps the home in its mission
is through a service of dedication. The parents, sometimes together
with the children, decide on the kind of service, which may take
many forms. The Bryans wrote theirs and then mailed a copy to
each of the members so that the others would be aware of the
pledges they had made during a dedication which ended with their
own prayer:

Oh Thou, who hast ordained us to be all one family, help us never to
isolate this home from the church and the community. Grant that we
may give our love not only to those whom it is natural to love, but to all
whom Thou dost send to us. We dedicate this home to Thee, O God, that
by its worship and by its witness, it may help to hasten the day when
Thy will shall be done on earth as it is in heaven.

The little company that gathered for another home dedication
had each been told in advance what to pray for during the time of
intercession. One person prayed that those in the house would
know faith, another courage, another love, patience, and simplicity,
until each person in a simple one- or two-line sentence had prayed
for that home a special blessing.

In yet another dedication the participants moved through the
house, a different person praying for each room. All the aspects of
living—sleeping, eating, studying, recreation, entertaining—were
in the prayers for that house.

In our homes, using the ordinary events of the day, we try to
acquaint our children with a way of life. Here they will learn that
we belong to one another, that we share our joys, bear one another's
burdens, confess our dark feelings, and seek each other's counsel.

Yolande Ford told us how a difficult time in her home helped to nurture her five-year-old Arnie in the concept of Christian community. She and her husband had been counseling with Gordon on concerns that were causing them unrest. The little boy was picking up some of their anxiety. When his parents had a conference with Gordon, they always let Arnie know that they were talking to Gordon because they had things which bothered them, and that when they were troubled they first talked to Jesus about it, and then they talked to Gordon about it.

One day Arnie said,

"I want to talk to Gordon. I have things I want to tell him."

His mother thought that he was imitating what he had heard them say and dismissed it with some casual response. But during the next two weeks he began to repeat the request in many ways.

"Does Gordon talk to everybody? Is Gordon's office open on Sunday? After big church does Gordon come out? Would Gordon talk to me if he saw me at Dayspring?"

His mother began to know that this was not a passing childish fancy and she called Gordon and arranged for a conference time. When she told Arnie he looked as though a huge weight had been lifted. He was quiet and sober on the way to church.

"What are you thinking about, Arnie?"

"The things I want to tell Gordon."

The child spent two minutes with Gordon. Two minutes that were much too positive. He could say only the good things. He had a new baby sister. He had new shoes, and he had been to visit his grandmother. Gordon began to sense that it would be more helpful to Arnie if his mother were there, and he suggested this. Arnie ran for his mother. Back again with Gordon and his mother he was able to talk about his own deep feelings, the things which made him anxious.

"I feel anxious when Mother and Daddy and Dianne are away from me." He was not left alone, and his mother realized that he was feeling separated from the core of the family when they talked and played with the baby upstairs. Arnie had other problems with

this new baby. She had altered considerably the atmosphere of the
house for him. He was always told to keep quiet. The ordinary
noises of a small boy were disturbing to a baby.

"I told Mommy I have to do that [make noise]." Here he looked
at Gordon. "I want you to tell Elizabeth-Anne [his Sunday school
teacher] about that too."

Arnie cleared up other things in the interview. He did not feel
as much loved as the new baby. When he got it all unloaded, he
said,

"Now, Mommy, you tell your things."

At the conclusion of the session the three prayed. Arnie's prayer
was, "Dear Jesus, I had a very good time to talk to Gordon. I had
a good time to talk to You, too. Make Mommy love me more."

Thus ended a conference with a little boy who felt free to say
the negative things in the presence of his mother because he lived
in a home where a genuine attempt at openness and honest expression was made.

If we can make our religion a living, day-to-day experience for
our children, then the texts and content of Sunday school classes
become important and it matters what we do with that hour on
Sunday morning. It is then that the church confirms what is taking
place during the week in the home. Here the child builds a relationship with his peers who share his spiritual background.

A child is not enrolled in the church school unless he has a parent
or sponsor who will make this commitment:

I will attend the School of Christian Living or take part in another
mission of the church.

I will bring my child to church school each Sunday.

I will work with him on his weekly assignment and communicate with
his teacher weekly, either in writing or orally.

Similarly, the teachers have a commitment which they make:

Recognizing the call of God on my life to be the bearer of "good
news" to His children in the Church School, I commit myself in the following ways:

1. To accept the children and families of my class as my "flock," praying for them and communicating with them regularly.

2. To be willing to learn to use the selected materials and study and prepare my class lessons weekly.

3. To attend the Teachers' Training Class regularly and do the study required.

We do not ask adults to transmit to our children a faith they do not have, no matter how much we may need teachers or how much they may love the children. This means that some day we may not have classes for all the age groups. This will be a crisis, but we will not cover up the fact that we have a crisis by letting some lovely person come in and teach what experientially he does not know. All teachers have facts and figures to impart, but these are quickly lost to memory. The gifted teacher imparts his own love for his subject.

Classes are limited to eight in order that the teacher may know each pupil and his family. Communication between parents and teachers takes place in various ways. Sometimes the teacher meets with the parents of all her pupils, sometimes with just the mothers on a retreat, and always with individual parents to discuss their child and how they can work together to let the Good News sound in the child's life.

Teachers, together with parents who have a special interest in Christian education, are a mission group. The group meets once a week for worship, study, and discussion. During this time materials are discussed and teaching experiences shared. Always there is the question: How can we communicate the gospel to the children? We have experimented with various church school curricula, among them Seabury Press materials, Presbyterian Faith and Life, and the Character Research Project literature of Dr. Ernest Ligon. At present the group is drawing up its own philosophy of Christian education so that from this a curriculum can be adapted to our particular needs.

In 1962 for the first time we offered our class in Christian Growth (usually given in the School of Christian Living) on Sunday morning to eleventh-graders. The tenth-grade class is now a terminal class in the Sunday school. Parents and teachers know that the eleventh-year class is not obligatory. Thenceforth, attending classes is the choice of the children.

Another way the church maintains a relationship with the family is through godparents. They are an important bridge between the child and the larger Christian fellowship—a specific point at which the child can experience the church with adults other than his parents. We do not want the godparent to be merely a person who can always be counted on for a Christmas or birthday gift, but the one who will watch over the child spiritually.

We have found our days to be so crowded that we enter into few relationships not specifically planned for. Our godchildren are no exception. Because of this we are thinking of setting aside one day a month as godparent Sunday—a day when all godparents will include godchildren in their day.

We have also considered letting each child during his teen-age years make his own selection of godparents to fill the role of spiritual directors to him, which is the real concept of godparents. This plan seems to have merit for many reasons. Godparents, who are to be the bridge between the child and the church, often move away or the association with the home is broken in other ways. The godparents were originally chosen because of a spiritual affinity with the parents, an affinity which the child does not always share as he grows into adolescence. He needs to establish his independence, and this often takes the form of rebellion against parents and friends of parents. It is a time when a child needs an adult confidant, but usually he will not have it unless we can make it natural and easy for him to choose that adult who will be his special friend. One of our small boys commented on the church, "I like it because it is the only place where I have adults for friends." Children usually do like adults for friends, and adults covet the friendship of a child. This would simply be a way of confessing what is in our hearts, and letting it be.

This asks a kind of maturity which we do not always have. Will parents help a child move into friendships with other adults? There is a dying unto self in this, for it says what is pain for a parent to know: that others can give to his child what he cannot give. This is always true, but it is hard for every parent to accept. This plan even promises to be difficult for godparents who will not like giving up the role to others. But surely the day that a child sets out from his father's house toward a new land is a day touched by grace for those who bid him Godspeed.

Another means whereby the church can strengthen the religious life of the home was introduced into our 1962 program: retreats for Junior High students and teen-agers. In structure they have followed those that we have for adults, with specific periods of instruction, meditation, and silence. Each, however, has been unlike the others, because the creative action of God moved through them.

The first retreat at Dayspring for the Junior High students began on a Wednesday evening. Five girls and four boys met in the Yokeroom of the lodge, and one parent and their Sunday school teacher talked to them about what a retreat is, why there was silence, and how they could respond to it. After a prayer period, the retreatants spread blankets in front of the lodge and stretched out to contemplate a starry firmament and to listen to music from the lodge. This "settling-in" time was not only preparation for the retreat but for the "great silence" which was to begin at nine-thirty when they went to their rooms. When nine-thirty came, however, no silence reigned. Figures scurried back and forth in the hall, shot rubber bands, exchanged important pieces of information, and behaved generally unlike retreatants and very much like thirteen-year-olds.

Worship was at seven-thirty the next morning; after breakfast the group met again in the Yokeroom and were introduced to the theme of the retreat, "Finding Direction for Our Lives." The Scripture reading was the parable of the pearl of great price. There was also a reading from the book *The Tales Christ Told*.* The children were then given three questions to ponder during an hour of corporate silence: (1) To what extent have I found the pearl of

---

* April Armstrong (New York: Doubleday & Company, 1958).

great price? (2) What does God want me to be? (3) Can we complain because of the price of the pearl?

They evidently worked with these questions, for the silence was kept. Afterward came a work period, lunch, and a rest hour. The group then returned to the Yokeroom for punch and music. This was followed by a period designated as "sharing time." It was a complete flop. If anything was happening in the souls of these youngsters, they were not at the point of sharing it.

In the afternoon, Gordon, who was the leader for the second half of the retreat, arrived in time to join in a game of volley ball. On the drive out to Dayspring he had pondered what he would say to these thirteen-year-olds. He knew some of the ways pressure could be exerted to get the "right" response. He even thought of some of the ways a minister is tempted to exploit the guilt that children as well as adults have. One of the prayers he said for the retreat was, "God, help me to keep my hands off these children."

That evening he spoke about God's love for them. He told them that no matter what they did God would keep on loving them and forgiving them. He would never let them get lost from Him.

"He loves us enough," Gordon said, "to pay any price for us. In fact He paid the highest price to prove to us that He loves us. He died for us." When he had illustrated God's love by several stories, Gordon talked to them about those things which keep us from loving God in return and prevent us giving ourselves to Him. "Jesus stands at the door of your heart and knocks," he said, but He won't break down the door. He wants to come in, but not by force. He waits for you to invite Him."

He told them then that there would be a time of silence and if they heard God speaking to them and wanted to belong to Him, they could either say this or raise their hands. He emphasized that this was a decision they could not make by themselves. "You can't become a Christian on your own. If you do not hear God calling you tonight, you can't become a Christian tonight, because He works with us individually."

In the time that followed six hands went up—six children out of nine. After a prayer Gordon talked to them about observing the silence when they returned to their rooms. "My room is number nine," he said, "and if you want to speak to me, you come and tap on my door." Unlike the night before, all was quiet. An hour went by before there was the sound of movement in the hall. When Gordon went out to investigate he came upon Gregg who said,

"I was just coming to tell you that I prayed awhile and I got very frightened, then I got quiet and I knew God was speaking to me and calling me to become a Christian."

They had a prayer together in Gordon's room, and Gordon asked him, "Are you all right now?" and he said, "Yes, I am all right now."

The next morning, on the way to the pond for morning worship, Ken approached Gordon.

"I want to tell you," he confided, "that I just said 'yes' to God. I really listened for His voice last night and all I heard were the birds and the night sounds, though I wanted to hear something else. This morning I woke up and I felt God had called me and I knew I couldn't say 'no.' "

This left only Reggie who had made no commitment. After breakfast he was given KP so that he would not feel pressured by the talk that Gordon was going to give in the Yokeroom to the eight new Christians. He told the children that the day before they had been Christians by proxy, and today they were Christians on their own. He told them about reading their Bibles each day, praying daily, and learning to let God make their decisions. He told them to begin praying now about the vocation they would follow and about whom God would have them marry, which would be the second most important decision of their lives. He told them not to feel guilty when they did not pray, and to always be honest with God about their feelings. He added further that the day before, they had not greeted him when he arrived, and that he understood this, but now that they were Christians, they would be taking the initiative, helping to put others at their ease.

Reggie finished his KP ahead of schedule and joined the group so that he was there to hear some of the cost of being a Christian, and also Gordon's explanation of the various forms of baptism. When Gordon was finished, Reggie said,

"I want to be baptized too."

The children all agreed that they wanted to be baptized that day, and in a period of silence they chose the form. That afternoon at the pond six children were sprinkled and three immersed. Adult members of the church were there to welcome them into the Christian fellowship.

They let us know, each in his or her own way, how deep was the experience. Ken Whitmore probably phrased it as eloquently as anyone when he said,

"This morning I picked up the Bible, and instead of its being a mumbo-jumbo of words, it was as exciting as a television show."

The retreat ended, as all of our retreats do, with each person kneeling beside his freshly made bed to thank God for the experience and to pray for the one who would have the room next.

In the days to come these children will have other retreats at Dayspring. Harvest days, camping days, and festival days will all be part of their experience as children in this church. There will be nights when they will work with us at the Potter's House and days when we will teach them an art or a craft at the Workshop. We trust that these times will cover those when we fail them, will help keep them open to love, and will strengthen them in their "running toward God." If ever they should lose themselves in a far country, perhaps memories of these events will remind them that a Father waits their turning.

5 Marks of Love

In the spring of 1958 the Bryans dedicated their home in Rockville, Maryland. Several months later they equipped the basement recreation area as a classroom and chapel. In these quarters the Rockville House Congregation began its life together with Rob Bryan as lay minister. The Bryans had made a long spiritual trek from the time they first heard about the Church of the Saviour.

They had become acquainted with the Cresswells, who lived in the same government housing project in Arlington, Virginia. Frank Cresswell was interning at Walter Reed Hospital; Rob was just out of the Army and intent on completing work for a degree in foreign service. Dorothy Cresswell invited Lou Bryan to attend Mrs. Campbell's Sunday school class with her. In this class they heard for the first time about the new church being started. Frank was interested in the reports they brought home, but not Rob. He had been raised in an unchurched family and shared their contempt for all churches. Ambitious, cynical, anxious, he resented any infringement of the church on his life. What he heard about the new church confirmed his worst suspicions. It would not only infringe on his life, but its demands would go beyond reason. He had allowed Lou to put a quarter in the collection plate, and she wanted to increase it to fifty cents. He flatly vetoed this.

Somehow Lou and the Cresswells conspired to obtain Rob's consent to attend the church's opening worship service in October, 1947. The fact that it was held at four-thirty in the afternoon made it sound less like church and thus more acceptable to Rob. He made no comment on the service, but the next week it was he who suggested to Lou that they go again. Everything he heard in the next few weeks sounded so convincing that he decided to try for six months the proposed experiment of acting on the thesis that Christ was real. By the end of that time, he had no reservations; he wanted to make a total commitment of his life.

To the little group on 19th Street, Rob had represented the out-and-out pagan for whom the church was founded. They did everything they knew to meet him where he was, and avoided archaic religious terminology that might too early offend him. They were stunned when he prayed aloud using words that were steeped in church tradition. Then was confirmed for them what they intuitively knew: The mind stabbed alive by Christ finds itself at home with the great words of the faith. Sin and grace could be translated into modern terms of separation and love in action, but when faith gives them meaning and content, there are no substitute words that have the same strength. Rob had dug into the Bible and uncovered a new vocabulary that expressed the person he had become.

The Rockville Congregation has its ministry to the unchurched in suburbia. At the heart of it is a small committed core which makes the structure possible. On Thursday evenings it conducts, in the friendly atmosphere of a recreation room, its School of Christian Living. Attendance at the class offered each semester varies from ten to thirty. Sometimes a course is offered which is designed in every way to meet the pagan or the worldly person where he is. A popular one was called "How to Be a Free Person." Arnold and Betsy McKee came to this class in very much the same way Rob went to the early Church of the Saviour classes. Arnie was an organization man on the road most of the time. Betsy was lonely and felt resentful that her husband's business seemed to mean more to him than his family. They both thought the conventional church a bore. Church was not what they needed, but they needed to be free persons if they were going to live together.

In the Rockville Congregation they found a warm, accepting people with whom they could be themselves. The class material held them spellbound and they brought their tape recorder to the lectures and discussion. Soon the classes were not enough and they began to attend Sunday worship at the church.

Usually, nothing dramatic happens at the Rockville House Congregation, but every once in a while a life gets turned upside down. Now the McKees have their own School of Christian Living in their home in Racine, Wisconsin. Each week they play a tape recording of a class session for neighbors and local ministers who gather with them. They all do the assignments and have time for discussion when the recorded session is over.

The church-in-the-house is a first-century church structure which can have meaning in the twentieth century, but there is no house congregation unless there are persons infused by the Holy Spirit to go out under its guidance. We can discover the twentieth-century structures, learn modern techniques, and originate challenging programs, but these in themselves are not enough. They may win people to our organizations, but not to the living Christ. For this we need men and women abandoned to God, contagiously radiant because in their inner lives a conversation goes on with Him who is Lord. They are the people who fill one's soul with a free, spontaneous worship. Thoughts begin to hurdle the usual boundaries, and you wonder why you ever doubted. In their presence your spirit has wings; you sense the very presence of God.

The incredible fact that Gordon stresses over and over again in his sermons is that each of us can be such a person, not because there is anything special about us, but because God is life and to be close to Him is to have power and vitality and joy. These sermons are always believable because every once in a while we watch it happen to another as it happened to Rob. A person becomes new in Christ and all about him is the atmosphere of the new creation. He says, "This has happened to me! I know Him whom I have believed." One man said, "Everything about me is so new that my old name doesn't fit any more. I know why Israel was given a new name, and I know now why Christ gave Simon a new name."

When this happens to a person and God gives him a certain new power, then new structures become important because they are the wineskins, and one does not put new wine into old wineskins. But the new structures mean that the laity is entrusted in ways it has not been before. Each of the mission groups, like the Rockville House Congregation, is in a very real way on its own. A moderator of one of our mission groups complained to Gordon that his group was in terrible shape.

"We're not praying any more," he said, "or studying the way we should. We're just goofing-off all over the place and you have to come down and straighten us out or we're not going to have a mission."

"I can't be a minister to every mission group," was Gordon's answer. "Unless you can be their minister or unless God can raise up in the group another minister, they will be sheep without a shepherd."

This was a turning point in that moderator's life because he knew that there was truth in the words, that one man cannot shepherd more than a few dozen people. Each of us answering the call of God is given a little congregation made up of friends and family and neighbors. With this congregation comes the exhortation, "Tend the flock of God that is your charge."

Though Gordon does not try to fill an impossible role, he still exercises his gift of teaching to help us with our ministries. Ours is the task of helping others to be open to receive the gift of the Holy Spirit. In sermons and in classes Gordon cites the qualities of leadership that will help us to be enablers of others.

"First," he says, "a person must come to that place where he knows that the real issue is always an internal one." This is a difficult lesson to learn. The temptation of the natural man is to focus upon what is wrong "out there." Often those who cling to the periphery of our life tell us what is wrong with the church. Usually we can add many things to their little lists because one must be of the family to know all that is wrong. Perhaps a prophetic voice is needed, but if that voice has the power to heal, it will come, as of old, from within the community. This is the loneliness of the prophet: his words separated him from those to whom his life was inextricably bound. But often the need is not for a prophet; the need is for the person who can ask of God what he must do to be the one through whom new life breaks. "What in me blocks the coming of the Holy Spirit?"

Gordon says that he has the distinction of having presided over the deaths of more small groups than any minister in the country. He is probably right, and many of the times it is because there were not those who could be responsible persons. Again and again you hear a leader complaining that he is not getting the proper support. He becomes tired and sometimes angry in his spirit because others are not responding as he feels they should. He does not guess that their changing may be bound up with his own changing. "I am a man of unclean lips, and I dwell in the midst of a people of unclean lips" (Isa. 6:5).

If we are to follow visions, we cannot be overconcerned with what the church is not doing. The very word "vision" implies grace —that which is not seen by ordinary eyes. The following of a vision, therefore, means a willingness to be out alone in a strange land, confident that God keeps us company there and with the faith that one day another will join us and then another, and a vision can be clothed, which means for all to see.

The second quality of leadership is the capacity to take hostility. The mission group especially is hit by this not only from without but from within its life. In a Christian pilgrimage we can expect hostility. It need not take us by surprise. Sometimes it comes from our families, sometimes from our dearest friends, and sometimes from those for whom we have laid down our lives most sacrificially. But why does hostility exist within a mission group which presumably has the Good News and is committed to the task of sharing it?

The mission group does not produce hostility in its members. We bring it with us into the group and there, for many reasons, it is uncovered. The fact that it is a group on mission means that it is subject to peculiar pressures as well as facing circumstances alien to its life. Also, the Good News must be proclaimed from a community which has a life in depth, but this in itself creates pressure points. If there is not this life in depth, we feel guilty because we know that this is what it means to love one another. But if there are deep relationships, it means that our emotions are involved in a way that they were not before. This brings to the surface hidden problems, hidden sometimes beneath a gracious social veneer that proclaimed peace where there was no peace.

Any situation where there is hostility has the potential of being a step in a person's spiritual trek if that person has the capacity to receive anger without lashing back. We come increasingly to know that redemption takes place at infinite cost to God and at infinite cost to the people of God. The problem is to differentiate between persecution for righteousness' sake and persecution for our own ego's sake. Most of the time it is our egos that have us in difficulty, but this is no reason to eliminate a central New Testament concept just because it can be dangerously twisted. There is a persecution for Christ's sake. Hostility is the consequence of fear which has its origin in separation from God. It is thus known to every man. We must have the capacity to bear hate and anger and persecution because this is the cost at which a person is born into the kingdom of God. It is why Christ says, "Love your enemy, do good to those who wrongly use you, turn the other cheek." Unless there is someone to do this, there is no movement in a person's spiritual life, there is no mission, there is no overcoming of evil with good.

A third closely related quality is the capacity to accept another person where he is. There is a bit of the manipulator in all of us and a bit of the perfectionist. We tend to set standards for ourselves and standards for others, and to become critical if they are not met. We feel safe if we are moving toward our idea of perfection, or can stay close to the person or community which we have put on a pedestal. This is an idolatrous relationship, which is often broken when demands are made that cannot be met. We have superimposed on the community our image of what a community should be and when we are disappointed we tend to withdraw or to be critical. Criticism is often the gap between expectation and what we find—a root of bitterness which springs up because we did not discover what we sought.

So often a minister or leader will be halted in his own spiritual pilgrimage because he tries to be what others want him to be, or tries to conform to his own image of what a leader should be. Several weeks ago a group of ministers and their wives were on retreat at Dayspring. When the silence was over and the fruits of it were being shared, one of the wives spoke up and said, "I want to tell you that I have never participated in a retreat of silence before, and I didn't get anything out of it." Later her husband said, "It was a wonderful retreat. My wife was free to say what she felt, and I was free to let her say it. If I had felt her beginning to say something like that in our congregation, I would have been kicking her under the table." It was good that there was a time when they could be themselves, but it is tragic that in the congregation where they live out their days they feel a demand to be other than who they are.

We need to accept ourselves and we need to accept others. God is the creator. In His hands is the timetable, and we don't have to act as though we held it.

A fourth quality of leadership is the perspective which enables us to sort the little issues from the big ones. Sometimes we expand the little issues out of all proportion, thinking that in so doing we are maintaining our individuality and integrity as persons. One friend told us of a church meeting where the time of six people was used for one hour in a discussion of whether or not to have the piano tuned. This is loss of perspective. We let the little issues act as smoke screens which keep us from seeing the big issues and becoming involved in them. The leader with the marks of the reconciler will know how to listen to opposing viewpoints and how to affirm each person so that there is an opportunity for perspective to be restored.

The fifth quality of leadership is a willingness to fail and to let others fail. This quality in Gordon is what has enabled so many things to happen in this fellowship. He is willing to take risks himself and eager for others to take them. Behind this is the conviction that if God does a new thing through us, we must necessarily be trying that which has not been tried before and there will be no way of knowing in advance the outcome. This freedom to fail means that from time to time some of us go off on tangents, but along the way there is a lot of growing.

Our security-focused world needs people who will let come into existence that which may possibly fail. Our job is not to be successful. Our task is to provide structures in which the uniqueness of each of our people can be expressed. What we do not want is buried talents. Lack of creativity makes for unfulfilled lives and for dull Christians.

This year some of our people are starting in Christian businesses and as always there are anxious persons about, who are afraid they might fail. Indeed, for every project that has got underway in this church, there are the cautious voices of the experts to tell us that it cannot be done. They said it about Dayspring and then about the Potter's House and now they are saying it about these embryonic businesses. It will be wonderful if they all succeed and we can give God the glory, but there is a sense in which it does not matter whether they succeed or not. The important thing is what will happen to us as we work with them, as we meet with success or as we meet with failure.

The sixth quality which Gordon gives sounds deceptively simple, but it is the one which is most difficult to meet, and the one which contains all the others and gives to them their significance. It is a deep caring for people—not just those who are important to us, those who can give us something, but for all people. Because we are the church, those who touch us should know that the church cares. Gordon sums it up, "Our mission is to be able to say convincingly to another person, 'I love you, and I always will.' It is just that simple, but also that difficult. Witness how seldom we do it for others and how seldom others do it for us. We will come to full life when we can say in symbolic or spoken language, 'I care.' "

From time to time Gordon adds to this list, thereby increasing our awareness of those qualities which will help us in our pastoring of one another. Without exception they can be translated, "Love one another."

Unless there are two or three persons with the capacity to love at the heart of a mission group, it is doomed. This is the need for every phase of our work, for every venture that we undertake. Whenever we sit down to ask ourselves what is wrong, or why it is that a project with so much potential cannot get off the ground, the answer is always the lack of inspired people who can channel to others the life of God. And always where there is renewal in our church, whether it is a workshop or a house congregation or a prayer group, one finds a person with a fire burning in his bones who can say with Jesus, "I came not to be ministered unto but to minister." These are the people who have come to the place where they have a greater need to love than to be loved.

7   *Growth in Love*

You shall love the Lord your God with all your heart, and with all your soul, and with all your strength, and with all your mind; and your neighbor as yourself.

Luke 10:27

Sermons, and talks, and classes elaborated on the vocation to love, which we knew to be written into the very fiber of our beings. "This do, and thou shalt live."

That which we willed to do, we could not do. There emerged here and there a charismatic personality, but most of us were children needing to be fed with milk.

All of us knew a call to commitment, but what our pilgrimage with a people told us so well was how imperfectly we had responded to that call. The witness of the Church of the Saviour is to a God who makes wondrous use of even the little that we give Him. This has given us reason to imagine what might be the miracles, if we could be wholly surrendered.

It is not that we are blatantly untrue to our commitment, "I unreservedly and with abandon commit my life and destiny to Christ." It is simply that commitment is never understood once and for all. It is a basic fallacy to suppose that the dream is always ours, the mission always clear. Participants in great visions are always in danger. Love can go, and it can go in little ways without our even knowing it. We are all children of Israel. It is possible for anyone to take the richness and the profusion of the gifts of God and look on them as commonplace. We sometimes take even His people for granted. I was reading to eight-year-old Mary Ellen Campagna the opening pages of this book. It was not that I expected her to understand them. I was filling in time while we waited for her mother, but the Holy Spirit was making use of the time. Those first pages had a sobering effect on the little girl. A whole half-hour went by before she commented on them, and then she said,

"You know, what you read made me very sad."

"Why, Mary Ellen?"

"I'm missing out on the lovely fabric." (She was referring to the lovely fabric of the fellowship.)

"How are you missing out on it?"

"Every Sunday morning people want to talk to me, but I'm in so much hurry, I tear by, and I'm missing out on all the wonderful fabric you tell about."

Mary Ellen is an extraordinary eight-year-old. The truth that she had grasped was that it is possible to live in the midst of God's gifts and never to claim them. But it is not a truth vouchsafed to Mary Ellen forever. Tomorrow she can lose it. However, the truth does rest forever safe with the faithful community, and the richest gift of that community is probably a person who from out of it can speak a saving word.

Love can go in little ways, but also our withholding of ourselves is often beyond our knowing. You cannot surrender to God a self you do not know. This was surely also in the design of community, that we might find ourselves in the mirror of that community. It was as we shared the common life that one unredeemed area after another came to light. The joy of involvement was interwoven with the pain of it. Raw edges rubbed against raw edges.

We know about love in this fellowship because here we find it embodied in a way that we have not experienced in other places. Here, when there is need, there is always a person to symbolize the God who is ever present. But darker reasons taught us of love. We found within ourselves envy and strife and jealousy and division. Inside, our little worlds were often in shambles because we knew not how to love. We saw what this did to us and what it did to the fellowship.

Before we had touched this church, most of us had chosen our friends on the basis of personal appeal, or because of common interests, or because of what another person did for us. Maybe we found them entertaining, or charming, or stimulating. When they stepped on our egos, or crossed our wills, or too often offended, we dropped them from our list. If we did not say aloud, we thought to ourselves, "If that's the way he is, I'll have nothing to do with him," and we chose a new friend. Now we were bound to a brother for time and beyond time. We resisted this kind of commitment, but the call to commitment sounded nonetheless and we knew there was only one Reconciler for that which was irreconcilable between us and a brother.

The bright and the dull, those who were attractive and those who repelled, those who delighted and those who stirred sleeping prejudices, the evil and the innocent, enemy and friend, we stood before them all with the command, "Thou shalt love." Our faint response was a judgment, not upon others but upon ourselves. Before the gates of heaven we who could not love were the un-lovables. The appeal was to the mercy of God. But if the cross depicted the kind of love that we were called to, it also said that there was forgiveness.

We are not called primarily to create new structures for the church in this age; we are not called primarily to a program of service, or to dream dreams or have visions. We are called first of all to belong to Jesus Christ as Saviour and Lord, and to keep our lives warmed at the hearth of His life. It is there the fire will be lit which will create new structures and programs of service that will draw others into the circle to dream dreams and have visions.

To understand this is to be thrown back upon those disciplines which are the only known gateways to the grace of God; for how do we fulfill the command to love, except that we learn it of God, and how do we learn it of God, except that we pray, and live under His word and perceive His world?

Not only had we found through the years that we needed to

keep our disciplines, but we found also that if we were in earnest
about the spiritual life, we needed to provide ourselves with a
structure for growth. Elective classes in the School of Christian
Living were offered for members, but for the most part we were on
our own. Teachers and assignments belonged to the spring of our
faith. Henceforth, books were to be our primary instructors, and
most of our real study as members was to be done alone. The mission groups usually have a common study and prayer program, but
these groups include persons in all stages of the Christian life and
do not usually offer a sufficiently challenging program for those
who have been studying for several years. We found also within
the mission groups that our interests varied.

To meet the need for structured study, each member of one
mission group agreed to outline a six-month program of individual
study. These programs reflected the great diversity of interests
within the group, and gave some indication of how rich and varied
the study life of a group can be when each member has the support
and encouragement to pursue his own special interest.

One member working in the field of public relations chose
Creative Communication as his topic because he had been pondering the question, "How does a Christian communicate his beliefs?"
and wanted to examine poetry, drama, the novel, and other forms
of art as vehicles of the Christian faith. Another person, who knew
already that her form of communication was sculpture, wanted to
relate it more closely to prayer and meditation. She selected the
Bible as her main study and sought to interpret in sculpture the
fruits of her meditation. A third person chose to read the biogra-
phies of the saints and other great Christians, particularly moderns,
in an attempt to discover the stages they went through in the
attainment of self-integration and simplification of living. She felt
that she would be helped and encouraged in her own progress if
she knew something of the hardships they had been up against and
could learn how they had worked through them to acquire the
secret of proper balance. Another person chose the theme of eschatology, and another the Holy Spirit, while still another person
embarked on a study of the nature and purpose of retreats in order

to learn the value of retreat in her own life and also to acquaint and tie in the needs of the group with the retreats that were being held at Dayspring.

Thirteen people in all mapped out programs of study, and no two were alike. Each of these studies had the confirmation of the fellowship as needed for the life of the fellowship. In addition to a weekly meeting when it is engaged in mission, this group meets monthly and gives the time over to two of its members, who report on their studies. The individual study thus edifies the whole group, and the group provides a stimulant and check for the members who have the opportunity to share their research.

It is possible that at a future time we will go beyond our own group and ask qualified authorities in specific fields to confirm a program of study. If we are serious about the ministry of the laity, we will not stay with the elementary textbooks with which we begin our pilgrimage. Too often the lukewarmness of the Christian—not to mention his dullness—is due to an uninformed mind. There is no dearth of good, provocative books for every stage of growth. Often laymen and sometimes ministers tell us that within their churches they find no Christian fellowship; but there is no one who is denied the fellowship of Christian authors, communion with the saints of today and yesterday, through the written word. The exciting people in any field are those who have live and questing minds. It would seem to us that an important task of the minister is to put into the hands of his people vital books of the faith. This means to come to know a people well enough to guess what might spark interest here and interest there—to know what will help the housewife with her task and the scientist with his.

The Union Theological Seminary in Richmond, Virginia, has a Directed Study Program which makes available thirty-three study guides prepared by the seminary faculty and other scholars. According to descriptive literature, each guide "selects twelve to fifteen books that give together a comprehensive coverage of the subject. The recommended books are mailed one at a time, at regular intervals scheduled to meet the borrower's need."

In response to our inquiry, Dr. Connolly C. Gamble, Jr., Director of Continuing Education, wrote:

With regard to the Directed Study Program, we make no denominational distinctions, and you are most welcome to participate in that program. The courses are intended to build upon the basic theological education begun in a seminary, but there is no restriction on the availability of the courses as between "ministers" and "lay people." Since the Church of the Saviour is composed of 72 ministers, we should be happy to serve any and all who are interested in the use of our Directed Study Program.

There are probably other seminaries who have programs to continue the education of ministers—professional and nonprofessional.

When some of us were new to faith and were surprised to discover that Christendom had books—so dim is the view with which the unchurched sometimes view the churched—we read so avidly that there was little opportunity for the Holy Spirit to instruct our minds. Now we have slowed down and have found those few classics to which we return over and over again. They are the books which direct us back to that one Book and help us move toward the new land—the frontier in the soul of each man.

We live in a world in which, for many, love has not been embodied in any person. We love our neighbors as ourselves; the only difficulty is we love ourselves very poorly. We neither forgive nor accept that stranger within. Most of us need, at one time or another, the assignment that Gordon gives from his pulpit as well as in individual spiritual counseling sessions: "Use half of your devotional time for the next six months or a year to meditate on those Scripture passages which speak to you of God's love and care." We do not have to fight for standing room in the universe when we understand that the hairs of our head are numbered, that our lives are held in the hollow of His hand, and that to the God of the universe we can say, "Father." This news breaking in upon the heart, gives us the mission to love not only others as we love ourselves, "but as Christ loved the Church and gave Himself up for her."

Prayer teaches us of love. Here again we stumbled upon a world we did not guess. Most of us began our pilgrimage in prayer with books like *Lower Levels of Prayer* by George Stewart[1] or *Intelligent Prayer* by Lewis Maclachlan.[2] We returned to these time and time again, but to them we added others. Perhaps more than any other author, Lynn J. Radcliffe in *Making Prayer Real*[3] gave us in five little words a key to meditative prayer: prepare, picture, ponder, promise, pray. The Quakers instructed us in the prayer of silence through a pamphlet entitled *The Use of Silence* by Geoffrey Hoyland.[4] We had not only the books of Albert E. Day, but Dr. Day himself came and taught classes in prayer. *Creative Prayer* by E. Herman[5] became a classic in our fellowship and another of those books to which we always came back. And then there was Evelyn Underhill and the mystics to let us know that beyond where we stood was the prayer of contemplation.

If we had heeded the words that were sown among us, we would be a church of contemplatives now. Though some of these words fell on good soil, most of them fell on rocky ground and some among thorns. Those who write of prayer out of the deep prayer of their own lives, give words that cannot help but be received with joy, for they speak what the human heart thirsts after, they speak of a Friend, "who sticketh closer than a brother," of the mystery of the love of God. But the reading of books on prayer does not make a fellowship of prayer. Some of us found that reading about prayer was easier than the hard disciplines that were the cost of the promises we read about. We came to know that if we were going to learn to pray, we were going to have to pray. Christ ever remains the great teacher of prayer. We learned that the discipline and training required for prayer beyond the elementary level were as difficult and exacting as anything we had attempted. We lacked consistency and often let pursuits with lesser promises

---

[1] Nashville: Abingdon Press, 1940.
[2] London: James Clarke & Co., 1946.
[3] Nashville: Abingdon Press, 1952.
[4] Wallingford, Penna., Pendle Hill Pamphlets, n.d.
[5] New York: Harper & Brothers, n.d.

come first. Those things which took priority were most often those things which were structured into our lives. If the time of prayer was not inviolate, it fell by the wayside. We also had our moods to deal with, dry stretches, discouragement. Many of us discovered that we did best if we had a friend who was committed to the same study and practice of prayer, but our temperaments and backgrounds and promptings of the spirit were so varied that we found that this friend was not always easy to find, which made us begin to think in terms of spiritual directors and to wonder if Protestantism should not give some attention to this matter. The period when each of us had been sponsored for membership in the church had given us some idea of what it might mean to have a spiritual director. We finally worked out a guide that would help us to establish this kind of relationship as well as to know the responsibilities involved for both the director and the person being directed. It provided the incentive and the help that many of us needed to embark upon a program of spiritual direction and we have included it in Appendix 2 for any help it may be to others.

The program of spiritual direction in our church is for those who want this kind of support and reach out for it. Thus far it has been on a much less formal basis than the guide would indicate and from time to time we revise our thinking as experience instructs. We once thought that the relationship with a director could not be a mutual one. The history of spiritual direction seemed to indicate this, but we found that it was not possible to choose a director from within the fellowship and not have a strong element of mutuality. It is our feeling that if this question were studied, the advantages would outweigh the disadvantages. For a time a degree of detachment and objectivity will be forfeited, but as we grow in Christ we will come to know a holy detachment toward the whole of life. The mutual exchange of hidden selves may be an essential part of our becoming. In the receiving of another person, as well as in the revelation of our inner world, there goes on that mysterious act of creation which makes of us caring persons.

There is no growth or keeping alive the fire within without prayer, Bible reading, and study, but these need the test of our meeting with one another. Not in our closets or in our studies do we find out if God's Word has found lodging in our souls. If the kingdom of heaven has come within, its fruits are in our relationships. Here is the test of whether or not we are people in communion with God. Ever those relationships judged any pious or false hopes we may have had. They let us know that no legalistic abiding by the rules would make saints of us. Always by the grace of God we would hear in our souls a redeeming word and by that same grace speak it to another.

8   Ordination to Daily Work

In June of 1958, Gordon was invited to participate in and to address a meeting of ministers being held at the Ecumenical Institute of the World Council of Churches at the Chateau de Bossey, near Geneva, Switzerland. The subject of the meeting was "World Evangelism." The following excerpts from his talk to that gathering are indicative of his concept of the ministry of the laity, a concept in which this fellowship has been nurtured.

The Gifts of the Ministries

Each person is called to ministry. The ministries will vary. But when God calls a man to belong to him and to his people he gives gifts for the upbuilding of that people and for its ministry to the world. Though there are differing functions, one function is not more essential to the life of the Body than another. Each function is valid and significant and essential to the healthy functioning of the whole. One need not engage exclusively in a particular function. One's special function may merely be the primary thrust of one's ministry. For example, though the primary thrust of the clergy's calling may well be the ministry of the Word through preaching and teaching, and the administering of Holy Communion and the pastoral functions, this does not mean that the ordained minister, exclusively, must do this. There is no reason why certain laymen cannot also share in this ministry, not merely as the pastor's arms, but as a fulfillment of their own callings. Some lay ministers are greatly gifted in the spiritual nurture of others. In our own congregation, with very few exceptions, each member has his little flock or congregation for which he is peculiarly responsible. If it be assumed that one pastor will nurture all the members, the life together in depth will be severely limited. In our conception each member has the joy and responsibility of ministering to other members in the Body.

The central thrust of the ministries of most laymen will be in the areas of the world's life, but perhaps the professional minister also has a mission here. His peculiar ministry will be enriched by some costly involvement in the secular.

Likewise, each member should in some degree engage in a ministry to the Body, though the emphasis will vary greatly, depending upon the call of God and the special gifts he has been given. . . . The principle of balance can help us from absolutizing our own special concerns.

One order of ministry is not eternally more valuable than another. It is easy to absolutize the significance of one type of ministry and leave the feeling with many that they are second-class members of the Body, important only as extensions of the official clergy. This I cannot accept. One psychological reason for this may be the minister's inability to be one among a number of equally significant ministers. He may need to be the center of a revolving constellation. He may find it difficult to decrease while another increases. On the other hand, the layman may not really want the responsibility involved in an ordination as a lay minister of Christ and His church in an industrial society.

One of the most exciting things I have discovered during the past ten years is this possibility of ministry on the part of every person. Sometimes it takes years of intelligent loving and prayer for this ministry to unfold. But with patience the most wonderful things emerge from even the most unlikely people.

I believe the primary task of the professional minister to be that of training nonprofessional ministers for their ministry. He will help nonprofessional ministers to be ready to grapple with the implications of rapid social change as this change affects their fields of specialized ministry. He will help them discover the resources of the Faith for their ministry which is much more difficult than ours, because it is not as safe.

This task will require a focused ministry. We cannot do this in addition to all the things we are accustomed to doing. We cannot do this and fulfill the traditional roles expected of us. This type of ministry will involve misunderstanding, pressure, and at times, hostility. But, of all people, we should understand hostility and expect it. When they say all manner of evil against us we should not wonder, as if some strange thing were happening to us. Perhaps this focused ministry will seem like a narrowing of our ministries. I believe the opposite to be true. I believe this to be the fastest way of winning the masses to Christ and penetrating the structures which mold their lives.

Of greatest importance is our own attitude. The new life of God breaks out most vigorously around people made new. There are substructures of our own lives (as professional ministers) that are waiting to be wholly converted. I see us as being the central problem. We ourselves are not convincing in our witness. A greater degree of self-knowledge is necessary. Why do we do what we do? What are our motives? Is our authority really from God or are we bound in other ways? Do we believe that the people in our congregation are as vital to the life of the Body as we? Do we give lip service to the concept of the ministry of all believers while being seriously threatened by the reality of it when these ministries begin to emerge? These are not merely academic questions; there is real threat experienced as the circle of activities in which we excel gets smaller and smaller. Unless we see the ministry of the layman in the world to be as of great a significance as ours, we shall ever be tempted to use him as a lackey in our personal fulfillment.

The use of the terms "clergy" and "laity" tends to perpetuate the feeling of a second-class order in the church. It is still felt that the clergy carries on the real business of the church and the incidental activities are delegated to the laity. Either a new terminology must be found or the old must be invested with new meaning. How designate the full-time ministry of each person called to the *laos* of God? Although it is not adequately descriptive, in our congregation we speak of the professional minister and the nonprofessional minister. The value of this lies in the eventual acceptance of each member of his status as a minister, usually with the primary thrust of his ministry being in the world. The acceptance of this responsibility often takes time, because old patterns of thinking are strong. But it is thrilling when it comes.

The ordination of a lay person to a ministry in the world is much more than recognition of significant activity. It means that the person knows himself to be grasped by God for a task that only he can do and which the church must have done. This awareness of God's call has grown out of searching and prayer and participation in various areas of the world's life. Ordination means that the individual's sense of call is confirmed by his own Christian community. We try to be as definite as possible as to the layman's specialized ministry. It is easy to escape responsibility in high-sounding general concepts. The world is a big place and its structures are tough and resistant to Christian penetration. It is good for the lay minister to discover specifically where he is to exercise his obedience. This specialized ministry, though extremely important in our thinking, is conceived rather flexibly and may have quite different emphases at different periods of one's life.

The structures of the church must be geared to implementing this conception. This newness will not emerge because we are eager that it happen. Nor will it come because we preach on the ministry of all believers. These ministries will emerge when the whole congregation is engaging in its ministry in the world and when the whole structure of the congregational life expresses this intention. When the structures thus express such an aim, a person in his first encounter with the church will sense that the church exists as a servant in the world. He may resist the church, and well he might,

for he becomes aware that it is a servant people and he is unwilling
to become a part of it. . . .

The structures of the Church of the Saviour implement this concept of the ministry of the laity. Our first service of ordination was
written by Betty Reed. When it is used, it is a part of the Sunday
worship.

Service of Ordination

Minister: While Moses was tending sheep on a mountainside, the Lord
appeared to him in a burning bush and called out to him, saying, "Put off
your shoes from your feet, for the place on which you are standing is
holy ground." Jesus embodied this idea fully, teaching that all ground
is holy. All of life for our Master was hallowed, to be dedicated fully to
God; all of life was a sacrament. The new "holy of holies," the new inner
sanctuary, is in each of us, for each of us is a temple of the Holy Spirit.
A Christian is on holy ground wherever he is.

Today,   (name)   has come to acknowledge to God and to us
that the work he does each day takes place on holy ground. He comes
to ask God's blessing on his work and for guidance in making each act he
performs pleasing in God's sight. He comes to give back to God the
work which God has given him to do. In turn, we in the Christian community come to offer   (name)   the strength and love and encouragement which our being together in Christ makes possible.

(Participant moves forward, facing the altar)

Minister to Participant: Your work and your worship are intimately
interwoven. In fact, they are not separate at all: Your work grows out of
your worship and your worship grows out of your work.   (name)   ,
do you come today to acknowledge that the place where you work is as
holy as the place where you worship?

Participant: I do. (*Kneels and speaks as follows, or in words of his
own*): Enabled by Christ's love for me, I shall endeavor to make each
day's work a sacrament. I pray that my work will be cleansed of all
spiritual or material selfishness, of all impatience or criticism, of all secret
desire for consolation, recognition or reward. Turn, O God, my seeing

into loving, that I may witness to the redeeming love of Jesus Christ for all men. In His name I make my prayer. Amen.

(Participant remains kneeling, and sponsor moves forward, placing his hand on shoulder of participant)

Minister: It is fitting that the dedication of your work to God be sealed with the strengthening devotion of your Christian community.

(Sponsor)   , by placing his hand on your shoulder, offers ourselves to you as channels of the empowering grace of the Body of Christ, pledging our love, interest, and encouragement in the work you have dedicated to God's care and guidance. Let us pray:

O Master Workman, Christ, how thankful we are that Thou has called out   (name)   to work with Thee. As he goes out to do Thy will, wilt Thou forgive him, train him, use him, to Thine own glory. Cause him, we pray, to recall again and again that the ground on which he works is holy ground. Light a burning bush of Thy love within his spirit as he takes his particular place in the world to do Thy work. In the name of the Father, and of the Son, and of the Holy Spirit. Amen.

Douglas Walrath, Minister of the Reformed Church in Middleburg, New York, told us how the group structure in his church helps to implement this concept of the lay person as a minister in the structures of the world. Their groups have ten persons apiece, and each week one person is given an opportunity to share his ministry with the group members, letting the group know how he is succeeding or failing in his office or place of business, in his home life, or community relations, as an agent of reconciliation. The group then comments on his ministry, giving him an objective point of reference and the support of the community he represents. In ten weeks he will report again.

In the future we will have retreats at Dayspring which will be in special fields of vocation—education, medicine, the law, the arts —so that perhaps God may speak a word that will help us to witness more effectively to Him.

We know that it is not our job to win the kingdoms of the world for ourselves. Nor are we to make them conform. We simply have to make witness to Jesus Christ and to Him crucified. We do not have to acquire power, though it is possible that we may move into positions of influence, but this also will be simply in order that we may witness. We have only to grow in the art of living and then in season and out of season to preach the Word in all the ways where we walk. Gordon put it this way:

This is what will make possible the continuance of those structures of order which are good and in which it is right that we should live. The world of law simply will not survive unless the law of God is spoken to the world of law. Government cannot survive unless God's Word is spoken in the field of government. Nations cannot survive in relation to one another unless they are in relationship with Him who binds all things together. Civilizations do not totter simply because they come to an end of a cycle. They fall because they no longer hear the Word of God. Nothing happens by chance in this life, and so by our witness in politics, or by our witness in the family, or our witness in the neighborhood, or whatever field we are in, we enable that order to live—that structure to survive. It will not survive without this witness which we make. It is still necessary for individuals to be confronted with the claims of the sovereign Christ, and to come into this life which we share as a people. Outside of this people of God, in the living sense, there is no salvation. This is our job.

We all have our different jobs, but we all have this one job of reflecting the love of Christ.

9   *The Potter's House*

We each had that job we went to as a representative of a heavenly kingdom, but deep in us was the growing conviction that this was not sufficient for the times in which we lived. The church needed to make a corporate witness as the world needed the impact of that witness. But how were we to testify to that which we had looked upon and touched with our hands? What were the rooftops on which we could in the twentieth century proclaim the Word of God? Within us had grown a need to give away our lives, but what were the ways to do it? How were we, who were called to be fishers of men, to cast our nets so that others might have fellowship with us and with Him whom we follow? These were the unanswered questions which had made difficult the transition to the structure of mission groups. We knew that if we were to take the gospel of Christ into Washington, D. C., our groups would have to be formed at the point of mission.

We discovered that one does not make up missions. One stands in readiness and in the fullness of time God gives them. They are not superimposed, but they emerge from the life of a people to help express that life.

In the winter of 1958 Gordon was invited to be the guest Lenten speaker at a church in New England. Mary described the church as "dismal" and the congregation as "shivering."

Gordon said, "As I looked on those granite figures, I had to repress in myself the urge to tear my robe off and to walk out of that church into the night where the air would be clean and I could feel clean. They had supposedly come together to commemorate a high point in the church year, but the only evidence of life was the tinkling of coins falling into the collection plates."

When the service was over that night he and Mary drove a long way. They finally stopped at a small hotel where the last vacant room was above a tavern. Noisy voices and gay jukebox melodies drifted into their room and kept them from sleeping. Reflecting on the sounds below and the church they had left behind, Gordon recollected, "I realized that there was more warmth and fellowship in that tavern than there was in the church. If Jesus of Nazareth had His choice He would probably have come to the tavern rather than to the church we visited."

The next morning they had breakfast at a small coffee house across from the hotel. The people who went in and out greeted one another, read their newspapers, and commented on the day's news. "We thought again," says Gordon, "that Christ would have been more at home in the coffee house."

Gordon and Mary reached home that night in time to lead our vocation class in its exploration of the subject of mission. In telling of their New England trip, Gordon suggested that perhaps the church ought to hold its meetings in taverns and restaurants where folk with questing spirits could touch its life. We spent the rest of the evening talking about the idea. We explored the thought of holding the classes of our School of Christian Living in the rented room of a restaurant. We reasoned that Washington had a lot of restaurants with rooms that were not used on weekday nights. It seemed logical to us that they would be happy to underwrite some of their expenses by renting out space for a couple of hours once a week. As Alexander Woollcott had once made famous a literary table at the Hotel Algonquin, so we pictured ourselves making famous (by the sheer contagion of our own excitement) a religious table at a restaurant. No longer would we have to wait until our friends were desperate enough to respond to our churchy invitation to visit a class in the School of Christian Living. We would invite them down to the tavern to hear what Christianity had to say at the point of politics or a discourse on the "Meaning of Persons." They might be attending our same old classes in Christian Ethics or Christian Growth, but these would be designed for moderns who for one reason or another had "written off" the church.

In a tavern or a restaurant of the city we would give the irreligious a chance to ask aloud their religious questions. Paul Tillich puts these questions as, "What is the meaning of life? Where do we come from, where do we go? What shall we do? What should we become in the short stretch between birth and death?"

By renting space in restaurants we would save tremendous overhead expense. Each group might become a church in itself. When it became large, it would subdivide and meet in still another restaurant. As members learned about the stewardship of money and began to tithe, each group would have the money that was needed for a dynamic ministry in the city. It could hold its own worship services in borrowed church sanctuaries on a Sunday afternoon. It seemed to us then, as it does now, that the times are too tragic to plow the energies and resources of the Christian community back into building programs. But how is it possible to do other than this when you are an evangelistic church and your congregation is growing and there is the legitimate need of space for Sunday schools and educational programs and youth work and other essential activities?

We have no pat answers. We have no answer at all. We do not feel the way lies in bigger and better buildings. We are grateful for those that we have. In America they give to the church of Christ strong bases of operation, but how do we move out from them to take the gospel into the junglelands of the nation? This is the pivot of much of our thinking aloud. What are the structures in which our contemporaries can learn to worship?

We never rented a room in a tavern or a restaurant. This might have been a way, but someone dropped into the conversation that night the exciting thought, "Why don't we open our own coffee house?" It was an idea that the group enthusiastically explored, but this strangely enough was not the group that was to give the idea substance. Despite the initial response only a few accepted it with earnestness, and when the sessions in that class were over only one or two pondered still the idea, for a long time called "the Tavern Church." But it does not require numbers to keep secure a dream. There were a few to talk about it and share the vision of it and pray for it, and then one day there was that person upon whom all ideas wait—the one who says, "Here am I, send me."

Esther Dorsey heard the words "coffee house" and within her leaped the long-forgotten dream of her high school days, when she and her sister and aunt had said, "We will open a coffee house for the elegant rich." Esther was one of eight children in a family from Virginia. It was a family of farmers and truckers who had always made a living by their own enterprises, and it was natural for her to think in terms of vocation. When Esther married, Washington, D. C. became her home. The dream of an eating house was put aside for a job in a government office. Esther did not think again of vocation until eighteen years later, and then she said, "It was all I could think about simply because it was what we as a church were thinking and talking about. When the idea of the coffee house was mentioned, it was my idea—I could not get it out of my mind. It belonged to me from out of the past as well as in the present moment."

We cannot tell you how Esther became the director of the Potter's House. We have held meetings on lesser matters, but there was no meeting to consider who would be the director of what was to be a dynamic new adventure in evangelism. Esther had had no experience in the operation of an eating place and the grim statistics, with which we were familiar, indicated that each year more small restaurants failed than any other sort of business. Logically, we could not consider Esther, nor was it logical that she consider the job. She had had nineteen years of government service and had planned to retire with full benefits. More than this, she was the most level-headed member of a large, practical, down-to-earth, security-minded family who had too great a need to be sure of where every move would place them, ever to be adventuresome. Esther was a rock in the family. She could be counted on for sound and judicious counsel in all matters until that day she got hold of the mad dream of running a coffee house.

No official group ever tendered Esther a business proposal. Just a handful of people talking and dreaming about a coffee house said one day, as they thought aloud,

"Esther, wouldn't you like to give up your job and be the manager?"

"Yes, I would," she replied.

Any new mission group of the church must have its mission confirmed by the Church Council, and the Tavern Church accordingly was officially authorized. For the next budget, the congregation approved an allocation of $1,000 to help a group, now twelve in number, to get underway with its mission of a coffee house. Of this, $150 was immediately given to Esther to enroll in a correspondence course given by a hotel training school, which she could take while continuing at her job, and which for the most part proved to be a waste of time, since most of the material covered was applicable to hotels and large eating establishments.

For many months the coffee house group held breakfast meetings before Sunday worship. These were times of praying and planning and dreaming aloud. During these months we searched for a name which, like Dayspring, would have religious meaning for us and yet not alienate the unchurched. We found the Potter's House in Jeremiah 18:1. "The word that came to Jeremiah from the Lord: Arise and go down to the potter's house and there will I let you hear my words." Jeremiah heard no sermon at the potter's house. He simply watched a potter at his work and saw how he fashioned spoiled clay into a vessel which was good. In this he found the message of God who can do the same with our damaged lives if we can come to know that we are creatures made of clay and place ourselves wholly in the hands of the Potter. It was the message we wanted the coffee house to hold for the city in which it would be set.

The medium of evangelism would be our common life. We

BASTOGNE, CHRISTMAS DAY, 1944: Battle-weary troops of the 101st Airborne Division are led in worship by Chaplain Gordon Cosby. Spiritual forerunner of the Church of the Saviour was the Airborne Christian Church, formed by G.I.s under Chaplain Cosby, whose wartime experiences decisively shaped his thinking and later ministry.

WASHINGTON, D.C., 1962: Minister Gordon Cosby leads worship in the chapel at the Headquarters of the Church of the Saviour. Begun in 1946 with a membership of 9 and a treasury of $30, the ecumenical and interracial church is still small in number, but its reputation and influence as a creative Christian fellowship are world-wide.

HEADQUARTERS for mission outreach of the Church of the Saviour is a twenty-five-room brownstone Victorian mansion purchased in 1950 mainly on faith and converted to church use mostly by dedicated volunteers. Today it houses a chapel, classrooms, library, offices, dining room, and reception hall.

ROCKVILLE HOUSE CONGREGATION meets for worship and study in the basement recreation room of Rob and Lou Bryan (Chapter 6). This unconventional mission group to unchurched suburbanites is one of the church's many pathbreaking experiments to discover the layman's ministry to the world.

THE POTTER'S HOUSE, world-famous storefront coffeehouse where six nights a week the church meets the world. Here artists and writers, shoppers and moviegoers, poets and beatniks, businessmen and scientists, gather to hear readings, see art exhibits, talk and debate issues of Christian concern. The coffeehouse is sponsored and staffed by the Church of the Saviour.

THE POTTER'S HOUSE WORKSHOP is a pioneering project to reintegrate Christianity and the creative arts. In the basement crafts center, church members and strangers can take "catacomb" courses in ceramics, metal craft, textile design and printing, sculpture, weaving. Kay Pitchford, Director, and Bill Shiflett are shown at the potting table.

DAYSPRING, a retreat center on 175 rolling acres of Maryland hill country, was more a dream than a reality to parishoners gathered (above) in 1954 to dedicate the first trees planted. Today the reality has surpassed the dream: Dayspring includes a retreat house ("The Lodge of the Carpenter"), an amphitheater for religious festivals, a productive farm, camps for children and adults, and miles of open fields and woodland trails. Plans for the future include a renewal center for the emotionally and spiritually ill.

would seek to embody the gospel: to be the forgiven community, the community which knows how to accept, knows how to love. It was an awesome mission to contemplate because we knew how poorly we would do it unless the Holy Spirit were working in and through us.

Over the months our group grew in number to twenty. We changed our meetings from Sunday morning to Wednesday night. The charismatic gifts of the fellowship determined all assignments. A gifted cabinetmaker built our tables, which were designed in many shapes, including the shape of that early Christian symbol, the fish. Our program committee planned programs that would raise important issues and questions, our interior decorators began to create settings conducive to dialogue; an engineer explored possibilities of lighting; and artists designed menu covers, while agreeing to make the walls of the coffee house one of Washington's stimulating galleries. From the beginning it was hoped that the Potter's House would attract artists, writers, musicians, and craftsmen, and that they might begin to learn there to identify their own creativity with the creativity of God.

The church, in which great art and drama was born, has not often in the twentieth century gone down the avenue of art to find the artist. Art has suffered from the withdrawal of the Christian influence and the church has been impoverished. In our own group were artists, writers, and craftsmen who, in the language of each field, would be able to say what happens when Eternity bends down to touch the common materials of their trades. Perhaps there might be conversation tables where one could discuss the relationship of each of the arts to Christianity or of Christianity to each of the arts.

These were the days of dreaming how to make the coffee house an evangelistic arm of the church. Our study was given to evangelism. Great trepidation was always expressed at the point of dialogue. What would we say? How could we be informed enough to engage in dialogue on the many diverse subjects that would come up? These questions were discussed many times and the answer which evolved was usually the same. Even if we managed to bone up on a few, we could not be experts on every subject and this was not the real need. The experts usually had experts to talk to. We needed to be a listening people, people who bore the marks of love.

Through the Potter's House we would say to the milling thousands of a great city, "We will serve you, we will be with you in the way in which you naturally gather. We are not afraid of you. You can come and see those strange people called Christians in the market place—not in their places of worship but in your own natural habitat. You can come and ask your questions. You can come and vent your hostilities. We will be with you six nights a week. We will serve you, we will love you, we will pray for you and if by chance you ask the reason for the hope that is in us, we will talk to you, but the talking will come at that end of the scale. We will just be there where you can find us. We will live a little chunk of our life where you can watch what is going on . . . see whether we know anything about the mercy of God, whether or not there is a quality of being here which is different from what you have found elsewhere. You come, and observe, and test us. We will not protect ourselves."

While we planned and studied and prayed, the search for the right quarters went on. Available commercial real estate in Washington is hard to find. The real estate committee grew discouraged and decided the only way to lick the problem was to draft us all. On Saturdays we met at the church and divided the commercially zoned areas of the city among us and went out by two's and three's to comb the streets. We grew less discriminating as the months passed, but despite this only a few houses ever loomed as possibilities, and there was no agreement on these. But there was unanimity in our feeling that we wanted that place which every person felt right about. We held out for this even while feeling a bit divided because we were not agreeing. Once we thought we had stumbled on the right place in an old warehouse. We were so certain of it that the day we found it, our group held its evening worship service there by candlelight. Afterward we wandered through the cold, unlit rooms which could provide space for a theater-in-the-round and any other imagining of our hearts. It was one of those magical evenings that really was never spoiled by the fact that even while we submitted our offer to the agent, the owner was closing the sale with another party. Now we look back with gratitude on that narrow escape, knowing that in that particular location the coffee house could not have survived financially.

While the search went on, we held trial runs at our brownstone-mansion church where coffees as well as plays were previewed and the larger church fellowship began to grasp better the vision of the coffee house which had grown in the smaller group. One by one the skeptics among us began to see what it was all about, but some never caught the dream of it until long after it was opened. The whole project was especially discouraging to the methodical and practical who wanted to plan every step and to have all the business and staffing details worked out before we made a firm commitment at any point. If we had waited on this kind of planning, this particular project would never have got off the ground, because the people who held the dream were not temperamentally the sort who could do this groundwork even when they saw value in it. Fortunately, our business experts were people of prayer who were able to free us to fail!

Our help came in many unexpected ways. We let the readers of our monthly publication know about it, and small contributions from ministers and prayer groups throughout the country helped get it started. We felt again our belonging to the world-wide fellowship of Christians. Ralph Talbot, who was still in Rochester, New York, at the time, heard about it and called to say he was building a Hi-Fi set which he would deliver and install whenever we were ready. The neighbor of a member responded by writing a news story which was picked up by a press service. Bob Manners, a lay leader in his own church, and the owner of twenty "Big-Boy" restaurants in Cleveland, read that story and wrote to say he wanted to be kept informed of our progress in order to assist us. We invited Bob to a preview coffee house night at the church. He came and gave us important counsel, including the advice, "Do not skimp on lighting," advice we have never regretted following. As our engineer raised his estimate from $1,200 to $1,700 to $2,300, we meekly agreed, although the sums seemed exorbitant. More than anything else, the lighting of the coffee house was to help create an atmosphere and make its walls a gallery. Again and again, artists comment that their works are never displayed under more favorable conditions.

In December, 1959, on a busy thoroughfare we would not have considered earlier, two of our group spied from a car window a large vacant store for rent. It was dark and gloomy and poorly partitioned. The garish colors on the walls did not add to its appearance, but it contained sufficient space for twenty-five tables and this was what we needed. We did not notice that the store was situated between a parking lot on one corner and a theater showing first-run films on the other, or that a bus stop was located directly at the entrance. These proved important factors in acquainting Washington with the Potter's House, but we did not consider them when we signed the lease. The one fact we were constantly reminded of was that three restaurants had opened and closed in that long-vacated store. Hearing this did not dampen our spirits. With much zeal we began on a Saturday in January, 1960, the task of transforming that ugly building into a room of quiet, rustic beauty.

The modern steel doors came down and heavy handmade wooden ones went up in their place. The fluorescent ceiling lights were replaced by an innovation which gave the impression of sunken ceiling lights. The walls were all painted, but that did not quite give the atmosphere the decor committee had in mind. To the astonishment of most of us a truckload of old, weatherbeaten barn boards arrived one day with the explanation that they were intended for the walls. Most of us could not see this at the time, but fortunately we were not "on decor." While we shook our heads, the boards were hammered to the walls and used to encase huge pillars that had been unsightly obstructions to the view. Bit by bit, to the amazement of the skeptics, the place took on a wood-

land look. Ian Cramb, who had made a stone bridge to span a
stream at Dayspring, built in one corner a garden of rocks with
water that spilled into a pond. All this activity attracted the attention of passers-by. They pressed their foreheads against the windows, shielding their eyes for better vision. There were scores who
followed in this way every step of the work. While the less adventurous lined the windows, the bolder came in to inquire and often
to ask how they might get in on it. Long before it opened, the Potter's House was interpreting the church for hundreds who had
never touched its life before. Even the neighborhood was excited
about what was happening. The storekeepers became our friends
and stanchly defended our reputation against any inference that
this was to be another beatnik coffee house.

Artists, discovering that the walls would be a gallery, came to
ask about arrangements for exhibiting. Writers and poets and actors who learned that there would be readings dropped by to make
suggestions and share their own dreams. We began to feel with a
new certainty that the church need not do the begging as it has so
often done in this age. It has only to be relevant to the needs of its
time for the spiritually hungry to storm its gates.

As everything neared the point of completion, a representative
from the health department came by and looked at our beautiful
boarded walls, and said the boards would either have to come down
or we would have to caulk every space between them and every
hole, and that then they would have to be waxed. He left us with
a mammoth job and the cheerful remark, "Let us know when
you're done." The Saturday and evening crews went back to work
—now with caulking guns, which few of us handled with any
facility. Hundreds of hours later when the job was done and every
board rubbed down and stained, we surveyed a room which was
even lovelier for this District regulation and decided again that
"all things work together for good. . . ."

Our inspector friend returned even more stern of countenance
and moved from place to place with his flashlight. Finally he gave
his O.K. and wrote the paper that would secure us a license. Only

then did he say, "It's a nice place you have here," and consent to take a menu. Our hearts fell again, however, when he paused outside to study the pond in the window.

"The water hasn't been running today," Esther said, "and he'll probably say it's stagnant."

He walked back and forth in front of the window as though he did not know whether to come back in or go on. Finally he came in.

"About that fountain," he said. "I have an alligator, about so long, and I would like to give it to you for your pond. It eats only one goldfish a day."

In one of the windows we placed a potter's wheel, symbol of our mission, but also for the actual turning of clay pots. In the other window wooden shelves were built to display the work of local craftsmen and around the room was placed sculpture and art work. In rehearsal for opening week was Edna St. Vincent Millay's *Aria Da Capo,* a play dealing with relationships which broke down because communication was poor. Perhaps in time the coffee house crowd would come to know that this was a place of creativity.

The Potter's House opened to the public in April, 1960. The first weeks were exciting, promising, and exhausting. All kinds of people came, from a barefoot girl to a count and countess. Almost everyone sensed that there was something different about this coffee house and their comments were expressed in many ways. There were the three college students who spent twenty-five cents each during the whole of an evening, but hoped so much that we would make a go of it because "it was the one place in Washington where they could feel a peace." There were the bearded and leotarded representatives of the beatniks who came to scoff, and sat orderly and receptive. There was the woman Mary Cosby spilled water on, and then made friends with as she dried her out over the washroom blower. There was the minister who came with his Bible ready "to preach the Word" and went home to weep because, he wrote, "I was forced to read a new book which said, 'Go down to the potter's house and there I will cause you to hear the words of Edna St. Vincent Millay.' "

The press was on hand the first weeks to cover the story of the

Potter's House. Art editors, real estate representatives, and feature writers found that herein was news for their readers. This in itself meant something to us, for we wanted the church to be doing that which was interesting to those outside its own doors.

It was not long before every night found all the tables taken, and on Friday and Saturday evenings the world stood ten and twenty deep at our doors. Despite the noise and clatter of a busy evening we still hear most often the comment that there is a peace in the Potter's House not found in other places. There is still no religious symbol to let the world know that the church is at the heart of it, but the winds of God blow, nonetheless. Wherever two or three gather in His name, there He is. The crowd senses this. They know now the answer to that early question, "Who is behind this place?" They come now to check on the rumor that there is something different about the Potter's House.

Artists, writers, beatniks, scientists, businessmen, politicians— all are among the coffee house crowd. Some linger long hours and talk of many things. Some wait months before asking a question. There are others who find it just a good place to bring a date. We cannot guess what they will remember of their visits in another day. We had one friend who left our congregation because he could not tolerate a coffee house. Months later he came to visit it, and said, "I've been debating the question, 'To be or not to be' and I was on my way to a bar when I thought of the Potter's House. I've just come down to be with you."

The Potter's House ministers not only to the world but to the church. Our own people know that when doubts and loss and sorrow and joy must be shared, they will find at the Potter's House those who can accompany them on a common pilgrimage.

This is not only true of our church, but it is true also of the church at large. An average of thirty ministers visit us each month. Many bring with them their lay leaders and young people's groups. Most come because they are grappling with the problem of the renewal of the Christian Church in our time. Some feel imprisoned in their million-dollar structures, smothered by organization, their energies sapped by committee meetings and building drives and membership campaigns. Others bring friends because the coffee house helps them communicate what cannot be said wholly in words. They know that the answer does not lie in a coffee house for every church, but they feel that there is something comparable for their church in its peculiar situation, and in the Potter's House they find the inspiration and encouragement to think aloud.

Representative of our visitors was a minister who came one evening with members of his church's building-program committee. During the evening, various members of the Potter's House talked with them. When the group left, a spokesman said, "We've already hired a fund-raising organization, but we're going home and call it off. We felt uneasy in our spirits before we came, and now we know that before we do anything we must look again at what it means to be the church." Another minister said, "I learned here what I was never taught in seminary: what it is to be a servant people." We remember this on the nights we are too busy to be with new friends in the way that we would like and are inclined to wonder if we are fulfilling the mission of the Potter's House. Perhaps its most important mission is to embody the lost concept of the church as a servant people.

The Potter's House is an exciting place to be. One intuitively knows that in this place things are happening. It would be easy to write only of the promise and the hope which are there. But this is written for the church that knows at the heart of its life is a cross. No redemptive fellowship exists that has not walked the way of Calvary and does not walk that way ever anew in each hour.

In the early days we learned that the Potter's House was to be a classroom for Christian growth unlike any classroom we had known before. It sometimes seemed to us that our adversary the Devil was prowling around, seeking to see whom he could devour. When we pondered this we reasoned, "Why not? If the coffee house is any threat to evil, it surely merits special attention." A lot of our difficulty came at the point of obedience. We had not yet discovered that obedience to God, like love of God, must have its horizontal relationship in obedience to one another. The coffee house truly belonged to every member and every member had invested something of himself in it. Somewhere in the soul of each of us lurked the private and prideful thought that our own little opinions on its operation were the best. Orders were reluctantly given, for they were reluctantly followed. We were living on the basis of the church being a *laissez-faire* society, and it is not. Every member of it is called to be a minister, but the gifts of each are different and different authority is given to each.

The original Potter's House Congregation, in the planning stage, was only twenty in number, and in the first weeks of operation these twenty were needed almost every night. With daytime jobs this made for an exhausting schedule, and fatigue was added to the pressure of unfamiliar tasks and unmastered equipment. The beautiful, gleaming espresso machine turned out to be too small and could not keep up with the volume of orders that came across the counter. Waiters and waitresses became impatient and anxious, adding to the burden of the counter staff. Behind that counter, neat and ordered persons were often teamed with careless and unordered ones. Though this was unintentional on our part, it was probably well planned in heaven.

Temperaments clashed. The task was more important than the person. We found much in ourselves to be forgiven and much to forgive. There had been those practice nights before the Potter's House opened, but the drill and the mock battle were unlike the firing line. Many of us had thought ourselves sweet companions of Brother Lawrence in his "practice of the presence of God," but when we found ourselves together among the pots and pans we wondered if we had misheard the call to holiness. That we weathered those early months with an ever deepening understanding of Christian community is testimony to the life of worship and prayer out of which had come the dream of the Potter's House. If we had not known before, we knew now with Dietrich Bonhoeffer that we cannot "live by our own words and deeds, but only by that one Word and Deed which really binds us together—the forgiveness of sins in Jesus Christ."

The little espresso machine that seemed so big has been replaced by one three times its size, and some of the little problems that seemed large have been replaced by others three times their size. But in the midst of them we have quieter spirits. We are learning to be more firm with one another, and also to be more gentle. We know the Potter's House now not only as a thrust into the world, but as a schoolroom where we can grow in Christ and into the lives of one another.

We discovered that we could not keep the beauty of order unless there were those under whose direction we would serve. We learned also the importance of this to the growth of each of us in our obedience to God. The moderator for each night was given the charge of Timothy "to teach and urge the duties" involved in each task of the Potter's House, to give direction "without favor, doing nothing from partiality."

Out of these early months came the covenant for participation in the Potter's House Congregation for members and associate members. Many of these persons were also members of the Church of the Saviour, living under the church's commitment with an added discipline peculiar to the mission of the Potter's House. The Rule of the Members of the Potter's House reads:

Friend, you declare by your membership in the Congregation of the Potter's House that the God of our Lord Jesus Christ, who has called you to belong to Him, has called you also to be on mission to His world through this venture of His church. As the word of the Lord came to Jeremiah saying, "Go down to the potter's house and there I will cause you to hear My word," so from on high must you have heard this voice, watched the potter at his work, seen how the clay was spoiled in his hand and how he took it and made another vessel as seemed good to him to do; and then heard deep within, God saying, "Friend, can I not do with you as the potter has done? Behold, like the clay in the potter's hand, so are you in My hand." Your life is to be so yielded to the hand of the Potter that you shall be to those who gather in the Potter's House the bearer of this message, a witness to God's redeeming love in Jesus Christ.

Associate membership is for those who are not yet members of the Church of the Saviour but who have had two or more courses

in its School of Christian Living and who share the church's life
and spirit as well as the mission of the Potter's House.

The Rule of the Potter's House for its associate members reads:

You declare by your associate membership in the Congregation of the
Potter's House your hunger for God in Christ and your belief that you
can best come to know Him as you share in the common life of His people. You no longer belong to the number of those who have never heard
the words of Christ nor touched the church of Christ. The Congregation
of the Potter's House is part of His Body. Christ is the Head of this
people. He is in the midst of them, but He is also out yonder in His
world. To share in the common life of this community is to share in a
life of worship, prayer and study—a life of loving and of giving.

There is another category of supporting members. In this group
are those who help with the staffing once a month or those who
are on emergency call. The members in this category usually have
a primary commitment to another mission group.

There is a sense in which all the working hours are for growth in
the life of the spirit, but there is a time of retreat before the coffee
house opens each evening, which helps make this possible. It is in
that hour that one can also see most deeply into the mystery at its
heart. The Potter's House seems in that time a thousand miles removed from the traffic outside its doors. Its wooded interior is sug-
gestive of a chapel that one might come upon in a forest. The
candles burn on the tables like altar candles and the spaces between
the tables are, for some, short aisles of prayer.

This is the hour when those who staff the coffee house meet for
worship, prayer, and study. Each night ten or more persons are
committed to be present on a regular basis. These are people of
varying backgrounds, ages, races, temperaments, and interests. A
casual glance reveals that no human affinities could have drawn this
group together. This is a community that would not exist if there
was not One who had lived and died and risen to be the living
Christ. No one belongs to this group who has not felt His call
and had that call confirmed by the group.

The study for each night varies; several groups are concentrating on meditative prayer, and part of the hour is given to sharing the insights that have come out of a half-hour daily meditation. Another group is reading Douglas Steere's *On Beginning from Within*,* and still another, Fritz Kunkel's *In Search of Maturity*.† The emergence of a relevant study can be illustrated by one night's discussion of agape love. Group members discovered that they differed at important points in their definition of agape. The conversation went fairly peacefully until one of the participants made the flat statement that he had no love for anyone in the group and no one in the group had any real love for him. "We're buddy-buddies," he said, "until we step on each other and then we're like any other group in any other place."

After the clamor of protests and arguments subsided the discussion moved into a deeper consideration of relationships within the group. The conclusion was reached that there was too little expression of the agape love of the cross. Members faced themselves at new levels and a few were genuinely shocked to discover that they were backing away from relationships in depth. "Love one another as I have loved you" in the concrete situation was proving a hard command. The group decided to look at and confess those things which keep us all from loving: fear, guilt, loneliness, idolatry, false self-concept. The scriptural theme for the ensuing twelve weeks was a parable or biblical personage in which one of these obstacles to loving was portrayed. Books by Erich ʾromm, Paul Tournier, Paul Tillich, and Reinhold Niebuhr were all on the reference list with other, easier reading.

One presentation stimulated such thoughtful exchange that we used it as the basis of a conversation table which was open to anyone in the Potter's House who wanted to participate. When the coffee house closed that night there was still a little gathering of people discussing the issues which had been raised.

There have been other conversation tables since then, but this

---

* New York: Harper & Brothers, 1943.
† New York: Charles Scribner's Sons, 1948.

still remains a relatively unexplored area with us. We look toward that time when there will be conversation tables concerned with social and political issues as well as with other subjects. We hope also that one day there will emerge from the Potter's House Congregation a company of players who can present every week a program that will raise questions which have eternal meaning. These are dreams which await a person who can give them shape and substance. They are dreams which will extend further the ministry of the coffee house, but we do not feel they are essential to that ministry. It is believable to us that if we stay close to Him who is Lord of lords and King of kings a miracle can happen in the spirit of those who come. It is believable to us that it makes a difference when we intercede for that Congregation which assembles nightly.

We do not know about the tomorrow of the Potter's House. Sometimes we have talked about the Potter's House itself being a work community. In addition to Esther, we now have two employed persons—a dishwasher and a coffeemaker. Perhaps this staff could be increased by several more and become the modern equivalent of a monastic order or work community which would make its witness daily through the Potter's House. We are not yet nearing this point in our thinking, but nothing is outside the realm of possibility when the call is to radical obedience. It is also within the realm of possibility that we will feel in several years that the Potter's House no longer expresses our life, and that we might therefore want to find a new structure which does. In any case, it is a way in which we can in this particular moment share a life and a cause and a love with those who seek after they know not what.

10   "On This Rock ..."

There can be no effective mission group without a committed core. This core is the church. It is comprised of those who have had conscious experience of Christ and have moved into discipleship. For some He has come in cataclysmic ways; for some in quiet ways, but He has come, and this is what makes the difference.

In our mission groups the hard core is the members of the Church of the Saviour. They have voluntarily adopted the disciplines of the church, and in addition, those disciplines which are necessary for the accomplishment of the mission to that particular segment of God's world where they will cast their nets.

There may be defection among the members of a mission group. There was in that first mission group, but the defection of one did not deflect the others. The members have declared themselves called to a specific expression of the Body of Christ and to be on mission with His people at a specific point of concern.

Associate membership is comprised of those who for the most part are moving toward full belonging in this church or another church, but they have not yet said, "We belong to Christ and we belong to you in Christ."

The members of a mission group must be willing to face the clear line of demarcation between discipleship to Jesus Christ and any sort of partial loyalty or commitment. This is a line which is difficult to draw for many reasons.

Often the talents of the nonmember will be vital to the accomplishment of a mission. Perhaps it is a mission in the field of drama. We have plays to produce and actors to be in them, but we have no director, and our new friend is a director. More than this, he has been a member of a church all his life. So we say, "Come be a part of our mission group. We cannot get on with our mission without you. It has waited your coming." Unless we have drawn the line between membership and nonmembership he will as a member of the group exert a certain amount of leadership and will help to determine the life and destiny of the group. Perhaps he does not believe in prayer, or his concept of it is different. He says, "My work is my prayer." This would not be unusual. We have ministerial friends who do not give much attention to prayer. Or perhaps our director is a person of prayer, as we understand prayer, but he does not share our conviction that discipleship to Christ involves our belonging to the Christian community, and that the purpose of a play is to draw others into that community.

The committed members must be the ones to determine the nature of a mission and their own disciplines as well as disciplines for associate members. It is surprising how easy it has been for some to participate in our church, to use it as an example of vital Christianity, never to think of going to another church, but all the while to fight that which makes the church what it is.

This is not to say that the associate or participant does not make a significant contribution to the life of a group on mission, not only in the gifts he brings, but just in his being. He often is the one who gives to a group its fresh, pristine quality, its eagerness and wonder. He brings those words that God whispers only to wide-eyed, open explorers of the Christian way, or he brings an objective point of reference, questions, doubts, probing words that need to be spoken. God does not confine the revelation of himself to a few. We know this so well that we are tempted to make the costly mistake of not distinguishing between the members and the nonmembers of a group, and so invite the uncommitted in to shape the life of a church when, if we took the care to ask, they would say they were unwilling to be the steel structures which support it.

As members of a mission group we need to be disciplined and we need to be willing to require a discipline of those who would be on mission with us. No person or group or movement has vigor and power unless it is disciplined. Are we willing to be disciplined ourselves and to require it of others when it means that we will be the target of the hostilities and the pressures of many who do not see the necessity? The chances are that we will give in unless we know that this "giving in" means that our mission group will have no hard sharp cutting edge, and will in time peter out.

This does not mean that we exclude a person from the Christian community. It simply means that we define his participation in the mission. We do not ask him to articulate what he does not know, or subject him to pressures for which he is not ready. The army does not take a man, put a gun in his hand, and march him to the front when he has never held a gun and does not know how to load it. There was one who begged that he might go with Jesus. But Jesus would not allow it. "Go home to your own people," He told him, "and tell them what the Lord has done for you, and how kind He has been to you."

The battle that we are in is one that will or will not take a segment of the world for Christ. It matters very much whether we are sloppy or orderly, whether we are informed or uninformed, whether we care or do not care. It matters very much whether we will stay with it when the going is tough. Are we clad with the whole armor of God or do we just have a few sweet ideas of what the Christian faith is all about?

We have had members in our mission groups who felt that the group existed for them and for the strength it could give to them and for the feeling of togetherness it would produce for them. These are the ones who in low moments say, "I almost didn't come tonight. I felt it would do me more good to rest." This is to miss out entirely on the evangelistic function of the mission group. The group does meet for the nurture of its own members, but it also meets in order that God may have an instrument through which His power may come and through which His life may break in new ways for the world. If a person has not grasped this concept also, he does not yet know that discipleship is discipleship beneath a cross. We have seen miracles in our fellowship, but we have seen no miracle that did not come out of sacrificial giving.

In our mission groups we should be able to see more vividly the ministry of the laity. Presumably the pastoral role is being executed by every member. While we require a discipline of nonmembers, it is not the same as we require of members. The members must give pastoral support to nonmembers who have yet to take the step into the circle of discipleship.

As members we should know those who comprise our congregation. To us has been entrusted the ministry of reconciliation. Our responsibility is threefold: (1) for one another—"consider how to stir up one another to love and good works"; (2) for the half-way church (associate members or participants); (3) for strangers to the covenant (those to whom we are specifically on mission).

First among our pastoral duties is that of prayer. This is where our sacrificial giving should begin. Have we prayed for our little flock all through the week? It is not a group of love which does not give itself in intercessory prayer. Too many times this has meant that on our way to a meeting we say, "God bless my group—let me see, who are they?"

Only the Holy Spirit converts, only the Holy Spirit redeems, only the Holy Spirit will make us one. A mission-group meeting can duplicate the millions of meetings which are held monthly in our nation, or it can be a time when God is present and forgiveness is granted and healing takes place. We need to ask God for the gift of His spirit on our gathering.

It is only as we pray for each person in the group that we gain the pastor's heart, and are enabled to put something of self aside. We will still see as in a mirror dimly, but we will see. As the shepherd knows his flock, we will come to know our group, to see how the various people relate to it—the members, the associate members, the world.

Members must not only give proper support to participants within the group and to those outside the group, but they must also remember one another. Many, though a part of the evangelizing group, will know times of discouragement or loneliness; there may be a problem at the point of relatedness. A person does not know how to relate to the group and the group does not know how to relate to him. We tend to assume that this never happens once a person becomes a member. We even go so far as to resent the fact that a member needs ministering to. We feel he is not assuming his responsibilities. He is letting us down. The fact is that all our lives we will be shifting back and forth between the role of physician and patient, of shepherd and sheep, of parent and child. If ever we arrive at that place where we do not need the ministry of another, we will have arrived at the place of not needing God.

Every member in our group is a member of our congregation. In our times of prayer we will learn how to be pastors. Our minds will be made alive to those creative ways of letting another know that we care. Our meeting with the person we have prayed for cannot be other than different. That little space in each day when we kneel before God and make intercession does the work of transformation, though for a long time it seems imperceptible. Sometimes the change comes first in me. The veil from my own eyes is lifted. I see that in me which blocks a relationship. I am more able to allow a conversation to reach profounder levels than the usual pleasant exchanges, or I learn to share with another the fruit of a meditation, or to make a telephone call that says I am concerned. We must move toward that day when we do not have people within our group who struggle week after week with the same problem and we are unaware of it because we are not the kind of people to whom others tell their problems. Somehow we must be able to make it known that another's burden matters to us.

Prayer gives to a life a listening quality and in this listening there is power that lets another's life unfold. We support and nurture one another by our very attentiveness. Conversely, a group is wounded whenever there is lack of openness on the part of everyone in the group to every other person in the group. Yet many a group is willing to be thus crippled. We have reservations concerning a person or we harbor a grievance, which for comfort we are often glad to share with others. To keep unity, each member of one of our groups has agreed to discuss any adverse feeling he may have toward another directly with that person. If a person-to-person encounter is too much for anyone to face, he may invite a third person to be present. In this way also we are to be pastors for one another.

While each person is nurtured in the concept of himself as minister, this does not mean that every mission group does not need a recognized leader. The responsibilities of all must be defined and the final administrative authority given to one person, who in turn is responsible to the church Council. This person is often known as the Prior or Spiritual Director. Spiritual maturity is implied in leadership, but it is also implied in obedience. It may mean that for the sake of getting on with the mission I will put aside my own little ideas on procedure or method or form. The more creative and individualistic a group, the more it is confronted with many directions in which to move, and the greater may be the need for one who has the authority to say, "We will do it this way." The practice of obedience has another dimension. If I can hear my brother and can be obedient to him, it may be that I will hear God when He speaks and be obedient to Him.

The writer of the Letter to the Hebrews says not to neglect "to meet together, as is the habit of some." A mission group, in addition to the times when it is engaged, needs those times apart. For most of our mission groups this is a weekly meeting which is divided into three parts: a worship time, a study time, and a time of sharing. The sharing time is used in various ways. Sometimes we reflect on where we are as a group, or discuss what is needed to move on with the mission, or articulate again our purpose for being. It is strange how easy it is to lose sight of a vision, or even of the truth in which we are grounded. We should all heed the words of Peter, ". . . I will not hesitate to remind you of this again and again, although you know it and are well grounded in the truth that has already reached you. Yet I think it right to keep refreshing your memory so long as I still lodge in this body" (2 Pet. 1:12–13, New English Bible). This is part of pastoring, that we will remind one another of those things we know so well.

The sharing time should also be a time when members feel free to share their lives with each other. It is easy, however, for a group to become problem-centered because it consistently wraps the whole direction of a meeting around one person's need. There will always be one who is low in a group. This week it will be I; the next week it will be you. Sometimes we need to share this lowness with the group or to let it know of a problem that we need help in working through, but generally we have found that this is better done in a time apart from the meeting. As group members we have unlimited liability for one another and this gives us freedom to contact a member outside the group and to know that we will be received with openness and love which is limited only by each person's capacity.

After the meeting times of a group have been decided on, they are no longer optional with us. It is elementary that there will be full attendance, although again we need often to remind each other of this. A little thing like two or three people attending spasmodically for a short time can finish a mission. It says something profound which has the potential of damaging a group. If a member needs to be consistently late or absent because of other covenant relations, this is something the membership is told about and consents to. If a person is providentially prevented from being present, his reason ought to be impressive enough for nonmembers to see it as an emergency. One cannot do the work of a group on mission unless he is with the group for its time of prayer, study, and fellowship. The fellowship gathered is not a means to an end. It is the end. It is the reason for which the mission exists. We simply want others to belong to this community in Christ, which knows that worship and prayer as well as service is essential to its life.

It matters, therefore, how we approach a meeting. Do we come with a feeling of meeting with a people who are "our people," a people who will share with us whatever is involved in the specific mission to which we are called—the sacrifice, the joy, the suffering, the fatigue? Do we come in gratitude for this little company, both those who are strong and those who are weak? This is a group which is embodying love in action when it meets. We are in that moment experiencing the fellowship of the redeemed. It is true that we will not always feel it, but by faith we will affirm it. We will proceed on the basis that something is happening, though this may be contrary to what we feel. We have already been found by Him who is the Lord of life. We are claiming a reality which has already taken place. Jesus Christ is present. There is nothing more to ask.

In addition to those times when the whole mission group meets, there should be times when the members alone come together to work on their special responsibilities, one of which is the nurture of associate members. Do they all appear to be with it, or are some not participating but withdrawing to the sidelines? Are there places where we can be of specific help? Is the structure perhaps too tight or too loose? Is the study challenging enough? Are there points at which the work can be strengthened or the burden lightened?

Also, members need a time when they can work through those matters which enable them to make a strong witness. When we are with nonmembers or on mission, we ought to be able to present a united front at the point of essentials. If we must differ, we should do it in a way that is upbuilding. There is a difference between the planning time and the time of engagement. "If the bugle gives an uncertain sound, who will come to the battle?"

Because members have a shepherding responsibility toward non-members and are at the same time responsible for the mission, it is important to maintain within a group a ratio between members and nonmembers. We cannot add to our numbers without having considered the question of how many people the committed core can properly care for while it is on mission. When we accept a person into our group, we are responsible for him before God. Can we be with him enough to let him know that God cares? Can we be with him at the crisis points of his life, and at the times he will need sustaining help? Will we help him to find that task which will express his life? Or will this be one more disillusioning experience: "You weren't what I thought you were. I was in trouble and you did not come. You talk about loving, but it's all talk."

We also need to be aware of our evangelistic strategy. Christ re-
cruits for His kingdom's sake. He calls Andrew, and Andrew seeks
out Peter. If a group is to minister to many different types of people, it must have within the group varying types. Otherwise we
who are so eager not to discriminate, do discriminate. We become
a class church, ministering to its own and excluding by its very
nature those of other classes.

The Christian fellowship draws from the whole spectrum of life.
We need to place in positions of leadership the kind of person who
touches the total—that kind of person to whom many different
kinds of people gravitate. Gifts vary, and there is a type of personality which is a special gift. It is not superior to other gifts.
Some have the gift of leading serious theological discussions, others
the one of giving the light touch; each gift is equally important.
The hand does not say to the eye, "I have no need of you," and yet
we recognize that each member has a function the other cannot fill.

Having said that each group needs to be aware of its evangelistic
strategy in recruiting members, we would also say that each group
needs to accept its inadequacy. We ought never to say, "If we only
had this person in the group" or "If that person were only different." We accept ourselves and we give to God our sinning creature-
hood and He uses it to His glory. Sometimes it is the poorly
manned, inadequate group which is the stronger, because it knows
that it cannot depend on itself.

Basic integrity and honesty are demanded for the upbuilding
of the Christian community. Therefore, from time to time we need
to look at the conditions of group membership that we have accepted. Have we followed through on that which we are committed to do? It is easy to become insincere or unreal unless we
have a time of self-examination, a time when we renew our awareness of those disciplines which we said we wanted as a part of
our lives, and which are essential to being a hard-hitting task force.

Out yonder lies the world. The time of "come" is over. The
church is mission and in our mission groups we have positioned
ourselves at the point of "go."

11   *The Renewal Center*

The early church believed itself commissioned by Christ to heal disease: emotional, physical, spiritual. It had no doubt of its power to do so. Total healing was the very essence of Jesus' ministry.

When we think of the Renewal Center there comes to mind the story of the paralytic whose friends departed from usual ways in order to place him in the presence of Jesus: "And when they could not get near him because of the crowd, they removed the roof above him; and when they had made an opening, they let down the pallet on which the paralytic lay" (Mark 2:4).

Can we do this for the emotionally ill in our day? This is the plan and the hope of our Renewal Center mission group. We will create in the midst of the Christian community a home for those who are emotionally disturbed, those who are alcoholics, those who need a half-way house as they leave mental institutions, or those who need a time of quiet and relief from responsibilities in order to halt a move toward a mental institution and perhaps to save long months and even years of hospital treatment. Not only will we provide the best counseling and medical help available, but the prayers of the faithful, so that perchance God may heal minds and emotions directly.

The location of the Renewal Center will be Dayspring, for here the community of faith often gathers. Here we feel ourselves in touch with Him who can and will heal. It is a place to which we go again and again for the renewal of our own lives.

Like all the missions of our church, the Renewal Center emerges out of the life of this people. We would like simply to say that one day at our prayers we heard God saying, "Whom shall I send?" But it was more than this. It has been over the years as we have prayed out of the depths of our own great need that we were given the mission of the Renewal Center. From the time of the very first radio program, which a men's breakfast club in Alexandria paid to put on the air, need pressed in on the little nine-member church. One of the people who listened to that first broadcast of Gordon's sermons was a man recovering from a hangover. He had heard too much before he reached to turn the radio off. He rushed to his wife and said,

"This man is talking to me. I have to meet him."

"You're an idiot; go have a drink."

He did not have that drink. He called the church and Bob Knapp answered the phone and invited Gene and his family to tea. They stopped their drinking to go to that tea. It was the first tea they had attended in twenty years.

Soon afterward, Gene's wife entered a hospital for a minor operation. Her friends assured her there was nothing to fear, but her reply was,

"No, no, it's not that. I'm tired. I'm not going to wake up." She never did.

Gene, living on barbiturates and booze, went to the West Coast. After several months, he said to his friends,

"I'm going back to Washington. I have a reason."

When he reached Washington he telephoned Gordon, and began as so many have: "Do you remember me?"

The main objective of those first weeks was to keep Gene sober. Every morning he dropped by the church for a prayer with Gordon, and every two hours on the hour he 'phoned him. If he was in trouble, Gordon always went to him. When, with the help of the church and A.A., he had made it for three months, he was all right. From that day on Gene ministered to every life he touched. He was one of those gifted personalities who impart to a gathering warmth and color and joy. Somehow one felt better just because he was there. The grace of humor and concern was always in his speaking, though the stresses and strains of his own life were never wholly resolved.

Two years after Gene came to the church, he and Elizabeth-Anne Campbell were married, and together they became the bridge over which many were to walk into the fellowship of this church. From jails and alcoholic wards and broken homes they came. Through Gene and Elizabeth-Anne and others we became a church membership acquainted with sorrow, able to comfort with the comfort wherewith we had been comforted.

We have held all-night prayer vigils for our members stricken by disease, and we have also held a prayer vigil all the night for a friend who was engulfed in a black sea of depression. We have learned that to need hospital treatment at the point of emotional illness is to have to leave the redemptive care of the Christian community. We know first-hand about the antiquated, custodial care of most state hospitals. We discovered that in an American city which has more psychiatrically trained persons than any other except New York and Chicago, it is still difficult to find a counselor who shows forth the "marks of love"—of a caring person— and that even when one finds such a person, he has no time available. We have worked long hours to bring a person to the point where he would seek professional help only to hear the professional verdict: "Whatever you do is all right. This person is never going to change." We did what we could and the person did change. We find shocking the promiscuous writing-off of the emotionally sick, and we find shocking the promiscuous use of shock treatment.

While we talked about this and other things, the need continued to press in on us. It even began to come through the ministers of other churches and they passed it on with strange explanations, all unaware of what they were telling us about their concept of the church. There was a minister who called about a drug addict to be released shortly from the District of Columbia Workhouse, Occoquan, Virginia. He asked, "What are the resources available in your church?" and we made reply, "What are the resources of *your* church?" He explained, "We have a strong family atmosphere in our church, and we would be uncomfortable and she would be uncomfortable." When you think that through, you find that it says something important about the condition of the church of Jesus Christ, who was the friend of publicans and sinners. "And Jesus answering said unto them, they that are whole need not a physician, but they that are sick. I came not to call the righteous, but sinners to repentance." A church that learns this at ever new levels finds a peace.

Once we were so concerned about those to whom, because of their very number, we were unable to minister that we wrote a paper entitled, "Maintaining the Ratio between the Well and the Sick." The paper said, in summary, that we would have to bear the pain of having to say "No" to some while we lived in the awareness of the many who had said "Yes" to us. It went on to explain:

Our "No," however, is always in order that we may say an adequate "Yes" to some now, and to more with each succeeding year. Ours is a fellowship dedicated to spending enough time with a person for him to become a ministering Christian. As we remain faithful to this call we shall increase the ranks of those who can speak a genuine "Yes." It is our conviction that if we were to try to meet all the need which reaches out to us, we would be answering none of it. In an effort to have a semblance of participation with all, we would move into meaningless, surface relationships where the creative word is never spoken. . . . This is not to say we will not welcome great need into our midst and spend our days and nights in the meeting of it. Love will ask even more than this—that we give something of ourselves in the service of those whose lives will never unfold. It is essential, however, that the ratio of the sick to the well be such that the other ministries of the church go forward. It is also only Christian that we do not say "Yes" to a given need when there are not enough persons to meet that need. Ours, too, could be a welcome to one more experience of disillusionment. The person would then become the accuser of the church.

This was what we said in our cautious, frightened little way. What sounded good in theory never worked out in practice. The sick we have always with us. The reason is probably the obvious one that Greer Williams pointed out in the July, 1961, issue of the *Atlantic Monthly* in his revealing article on "The Rejection of the Insane." "Most of us, in sum, are psychologically handicapped persons." What we have come to know so well is that the paralytic is not a figure who belongs to a distant century. The paralytic is you and I as we gather to sit in the presence of Christ. The reason we so seldom know our own damaged selves or the crippled damaged selves of others is because there is no place where a person can feel safe enough to be himself. The church ought to be such a place. Fundamentally, every church is a Renewal Center. We ought to be able to invite people to come see it, and not require them to conform to it and to find their safety in the same way they have to find it in the world.

Everywhere we look there is need, and as we understand the Christian Church, this is the way it is always going to be. The church which ignores need, ignores Jesus. We are probably never so much aware of how weak we are as when we pray for each other in the membership of the church. We know the uprisings and the downsittings of one another well enough to make us aware that in this little fellowship we have the treasure in earthenware vessels, that the transcendent power belongs to God and not to us. "We are afflicted in every way, but not crushed; perplexed but not driven to despair. . . ." Out of the hope, born of our tribulations, we would find a way to minister to the crushed and despairing.

Giving leadership to the planning and activities of the Renewal Center mission group is Dr. Frank Cresswell. Frank and Dorothy Cresswell were two of the nine founding members of the Church of the Saviour. After having been a part of all the restaurant meetings of the embryonic church and on hand to see it officially housed in its own building, Frank, at that time in the army, was transferred to Fort Benning, Georgia. He had always planned to practice medicine in his home state of Mississippi, and when he was released from the army, he and Dorothy and their children went to Aberdeen, Mississippi.

Dorothy will tell you that it was their intention to return to the Church of the Saviour, but Frank was not so aware of this. He merely wanted to care for the sick of Aberdeen. Frank was one of those Christians who exudes what Jacques Ellul calls a "style" of life. The townspeople soon discovered that they had in their new doctor a minister. A large practice and six children did not keep either Frank or Dorothy from being active in their church. Dorothy once said, "If ever I was home on Sunday because one of the children was ill, there would be an unusual quiet in the house. Our telephone which rang constantly was always silent that eleventh hour on Sunday just because everyone knew Frank was in church."

During their years in Aberdeen the Cresswells made periodic trips to the Church of the Saviour. On one of these trips they were with a group which was exploring what a church might do for the spiritually sick if it cared enough. Frank listened attentively. In Aberdeen he had discovered what all discover who have eyes to see and ears to hear: We live in a world of deeply troubled persons. He was learning also that the creative possibilities of his ministry could not be realized without a sustaining fellowship, nor could the ministries of the church's individual members substitute for the corporate ministry and witness of the church. He pondered these and other things, and in January, 1958, moved his family back to Washington, D. C. Several months later he went into practice with a doctor working primarily with alcoholic patients.

The Renewal Center mission group began to form around the Cresswells. The group early decided that the Director of the Life Renewal Center should be a pastoral psychologist with clinical experience and an understanding of the concept of commitment as we have expressed it in these pages.

Whatever form the Renewal Center takes, it is to be part of our life. Our church in its approval of this mission was aware that it was committing itself to becoming involved to the extent of being a family to those to whom it would seek to minister. As we serve at the Potter's House under the direction of Esther and the moderators, we will serve at the Renewal Center in those posts designated by the pastoral psychologist.

In the beginning we thought in terms of a new building at Dayspring with facilities adequate for at least twenty persons. One Sunday afternoon at Dayspring the Renewal Group met with small groups to interpret its thinking and to be instructed by the membership. It was an open meeting in which the Group shared its plans with the entire church body.

Those of us who had agreed that we wanted a twenty-room building for the Renewal Center were suddenly confronted with all that was involved in that decision, and it seemed to us a staggering undertaking. We were seventy in number and heavily committed in many places. We did not have enough lay volunteers to be with twenty persons on the basis we had dreamed and talked about. The alternative plan we discussed that day, of a small pilot project which could start in the farmhouse already at Dayspring, seemed more within our scope. The more we talked about it and weighed the advantages and disadvantages of both plans, the more exciting the smaller project became. We did not want to develop another institution. We wanted to keep the ill with the community of the concerned and to pioneer a way that would let other church communities do the same.

Dr. Granger E. Westberg of the University of Chicago had visited with us the week before and said, in memorable words, "We live in a society which sends its broken-hearted to state institutions. The place which helps most toward life is most like life." We recalled those words as we looked afresh at the white frame farmhouse which stands at the entrance to Dayspring. That day we informally and then formally agreed that it would be the home of the Renewal Center. We discussed how it would be out-of-bounds to us except by invitation, but that there would be no place at Dayspring out-of-bounds to those who would live in the farmhouse. There were newcomers among us who raised many questions at this point, and as we talked we resolved some of our own fears as well as understood some of our own resistances to the new responsibilities on which we were about to embark.

In the next months, the preparation of the church continued. A group of twenty-five completed a study under Chaplain Arthur H. Rost of St. Elizabeth's Hospital. The study covered the following topics: (1) some basic assumptions about deeply troubled people; (2) barriers to communion and wholeness; (3) resources for communion and wholeness; and (4) experimenting with group methods.

On Monday nights the group holds a prayer healing service. To participate in this service a person must be sponsored by two members of the mission group, for this assures that the one being prayed for has two persons who will be to him a friend. We will not pray and leave all to God. We will pray and our offering on the altar shall be a willingness to become involved in a relationship, a willingness to be sent out two by two: ". . . and he sent them out to preach the kingdom of God and to heal."

We knew that one of the primary tasks of the group was to secure a director, and we had been alert to every possibility. In the spring of 1962, however, there seemed to be a new eagerness on the part of our people. We sensed in our spirits that the fullness of time had come for the bringing forth of this project. We intensified our search for a Director. In correspondence with Dr. Wayne E. Oates of Southern Baptist Theological Seminary, Louisville, Kentucky, and others in the field of pastoral psychology we heard of the work of Dr. Joseph W. Knowles of the Institute of Religion in Houston, Texas. We wrote to Dr. Knowles about our desire to experiment with a distinctly Christian approach to healing and asked him if he would like to enter into conversation with us concerning the Renewal Center and a counseling program within the context of the fellowship of the church. Dr. Knowles replied that he would be traveling in the East that summer and would like to spend several days at the Church of the Saviour.

The visit of Dr. Knowles and his family was an exciting time in our church. We talked about the task of the Director and the training of the Renewal Center Mission Group for work and service. Dr. Knowles shared with us his own sense of vocation. He said that he did not see himself primarily as a pastoral counselor. He had had eight years in this role—five years in a psychiatric hospital and three in a pastoral counseling service. "I image myself primarily as a minister who has a mission to the church to help the church become the healing community of God in the world." This was the sense of vocation that we had hoped for in the Director of the Renewal Center. Dr. Knowles, however, was engaged in a meaningful place of service. The Institute of Religion was in the heart of the Texas Medical Center with academic relationship to five Texas seminaries and clinical pastoral education program for ministers in six hospitals of the Center. The Institute was on the verge of developing training programs in churches of Houston where both laymen and clergy could be trained for ministry. It was obvious that Dr. Knowles would not leave his work at the Institute unless God called him. He was open to that possibility and when he returned to Houston he wrote, "My prayer is that the God who dwells in mystery but who has chosen to make himself known in Jesus Christ may reveal to us what is in the mind of the Spirit."

Members of the Renewal Center Mission Group agreed to pray for fifteen minutes each day that they and Dr. Knowles would know whether he was the man to give leadership to this venture. When the group met at the end of a two-week period, members were of one mind: An invitation should be sent to Dr. Knowles letting him know that we wanted him as our Director. This decision was unanimously approved by the entire membership at a congregational meeting.

Several months went by before Dr. Knowles responded, "We as a family, feel the call of God to work in directing the healing mission of the Church of the Saviour." In that letter he said:

There are three areas in which I would like to become involved: (1) Developing the Life Renewal Center at Dayspring with the group, (2) giving some attention to use of present structures and finding if new ones are needed to give focus and direction to the whole life of the church as a healing community, and (3) the developing of a program of supervised

clinical pastoral education for ministers and theological students, once the
Renewal Center and the church is ready as a suitable clinical training
situation.

In January, 1963, Dr. Knowles joined the staff of the Church
of the Saviour, and the Renewal Center Mission began a new phase
of its work.

In that vast shadowland which is mental illness, there are many
lights which wait to be lit, and some which only the church
in Christ can light.

12   The Potter's House Workshop

It was not strange that the Potter's House should hold and keep for our church the vision of a Workshop where artists and apprentices and students could move deeper into the life of the Christian community. The artists in our coffee house mission group, in the tradition of artists everywhere, had turned the walls of the Potter's House into a gallery. They gave art a place in the midst of the traffic of a busy city, but also a place very close to the common life of our church, where it could nurture that life and draw upon it.

Sculpture, painting, drawing, graphics, photography, and crafts were all included on the first exhibit calendar. Most of these shows were reviewed favorably by the press, and attracted not only other artists but those who were interested in art. More than that, those who came merely to drink coffee found the atmosphere stimulating. Music and painting and sculpture and drama stirred within us all that creative urge which belongs to another world.

Over the years we had talked about a Workshop, but now the dream pressed in, demanding priority. We began to think in more concrete terms. We could do this because we had Kay Pitchford who is an artist and also a teacher. But more than these, she is that truly creative person who helps each one she touches to discover the artist within himself. Kay was the one around whom things began to happen. She was not primarily an organizer or an initiator. Others would have to provide these gifts for the project to get underway, but the first call was the call to Kay to be the Workshop. It was a call which had for her an authentic ring. It sounded in her heart like the voice of God speaking. She responded to it with a sense of incredulity. "Not me, O God. Not in this time and place. I have many things to straighten out before I can give consideration to this." But like Jeremiah, who heard the voice of God saying, "Tell these things to my people," and was never the same again, Kay could not get away from the insistent demanding from within. She was hearing what God is trying to say to each of us, "I would like you to do this for Me."

Like a few biblical characters before her, Kay said, "Forgive me, Lord, but I would test you that I may be certain." To the Potter's House group, she said: "What you do not understand is that I have family responsibilities and my salary requirements are more than you can meet." We glanced at the books, but the Lord put a veil between us and the figures so that we did not see all that was there to see and obligated the Potter's House to pay Kay's salary until the project could be self-supporting. Kay felt certain that after a year of classes the Workshop would be financially on its own. What we did not know was that it would be over a year before we would find quarters for the new Workshop. In so short a time we had forgotten the long search to find a home for the Potter's House. Kay resigned her job as an art teacher in the public high schools, and on the third floor of the church, with one class, the Potter's House Workshop began its uncertain existence. In addition to teaching, Kay did in the next months all the preparatory work that made it possible for the Workshop to open in its own quarters as soon as they were found.

The search for real estate went on, and month after month the Potter's House went deeper into debt to finance the undertaking. It was a time of testing for the whole project. We were determined to hang on if Kay would. When another school year began with no evident progress, Kay asked herself that terrible question which is asked inevitably some place in every project, "Did I hear aright, or was I simply listening to the imaginings of my own heart?"

There was no sign this time. Heaven appeared deaf and dumb, but the early certainty that the Workshop held God's call made it impossible for her to read into events the "No" of God.

These are events which belong not only to the history of the Workshop, but to the history of the Potter's House Congregation which was beginning to shape its own life as a people of God in the commercial, twentieth-century setting of a coffee house. There was every reason for the Congregation to want to secure its own life and to use any extra resources to establish its foothold more firmly, but this never occurred to it. It owed its own existence to those who had refused to be governed wholly by analysis and logic. It was deeply aware of the spiritual law that he who gives his life finds his life, and that this was true corporately as well as individually. The organization, like the individual, which waits until it is established with its own needs provided and its own future secured to begin a program of giving, knows a death within that dims its sight of the kingdom of God. It will surely arrive at the place of comfortable giving, but will it then know that there is reason to give? Will it have eyes to perceive the kingdom of heaven which is at hand? The New Testament says very plainly that God permits a hardening of the heart. In its financing of the Workshop, the Potter's House recognized that its own destiny was intricately bound up with the whole. It seems to us an important testimony that the Potter's House wound up its second year with a deficit in order that it might launch another mission.

The search for suitable Workshop quarters was complicated by the District fire regulations, which made it difficult to convert anything but a basement into a school without a huge outlay of money. We found that basement when Bill Shiflett entered into the search. Bill is that person whose many talents are given at the frontier places of our church's life. The basement he discovered had its entrance on the busy thoroughfare of Connecticut Avenue. Its front was deceptive and hid well the many rooms behind, so that we walked past the "FOR RENT" sign for several months before we investigated it. What looked like two rooms turned out to be seven, opening one upon the other in a catacomblike arrangement. We, who are symbol conscious, had on first sight that eureka feeling of "This is it!" A few days later we had a signed lease in our keeping.

A friend once said, "If there is an odor indigenous to the Church of the Saviour, it is the smell of paint and varsol." This time the transforming process took four weeks. The work parties, as always, were not only means to an end, but were in themselves structures of reconciliation in which we could learn to know each other and learn to give of ourselves. Some of our most consistent, creative help came from new friends we had met through the Potter's House.

A few yards from the Workshop the foundations of a new office building were being laid and there were the usual irresistible peekholes in the board wall around the excavation. But that project attracted no more attention than the renovation of a basement. There is something in a man which loves to look in on the activity of building, on whatever scale it is being done. So again we were interpreting our church to the man in the street. The newspapers sent reporters to do feature stories, and the Patty Cavin radio program and Inga's Angle television show invited Kay Pitchford and Jimilu Mason to talk about the classes they would be teaching. Jimilu, who is a well-known sculptress and designer, also told of a stained-glass window she had designed for a church in Colorado.

There were six classes offered that first semester: ceramics, design exploration, metalcraft, printing fabrics, sculpture, and weaving. The little folder which described them listed the tuition as $40 per class for each twelve-week semester. It also described Jimilu's and Kay's qualifications as instructors. There were two references to the church: one a dove on the cover, symbol of the Holy Spirit; the other this statement: "It is hoped that those who take these classes will not only find the hidden secrets of an art or handicraft, but the secret of the Christian community out of whose life of worship and prayer the classes emerge."

We determined that thirty students would make the new evangelistic structure of the Workshop self-supporting. When the first week of classes was over and the registrations counted they totaled thirty. These were thirty persons who had made a commitment of money and time to learn the discipline of an art or a craft. Now it was our job to translate this sense of commitment and discipline into terms of the kingdom of God.

Kay Pitchford, Jimilu Mason, and Bill Shiflett were our members dedicated to being the ministers of this new church quartered in a basement. In addition, five or six of our own people were enrolled in the classes as students in order to learn an art themselves, but at the same time to help with the spiritual ministry of the Workshop. To Bill Shiflett the most exciting discovery of the month was that all the crafts held parables. He found himself teaching in parables, because a piece of clay or old rock held a spiritual truth that came out in story form. Parables become a natural form of communication at the Workshop, so that "seeing they would not see and hearing they would not hear." Those words of Jesus which had always confounded us became clear, for at the Workshop we let everyone know that we were the church, but it was only to the person who asked—who turned to be healed—that we tried to impart the deeper mystery of the faith.

It is a twofold turning which is required, for the believer also needs art and the disciplines of art to open his life to the experiencing of God's spirit which is stamped on all that is. If he can look with the eyes of an artist upon a branch, or a blade of grass, or the wing of an insect, or the flight of a bird, he knows whereof the mystic speaks. He learns the art of contemplation and moves into an I-Thou relationship with his world. Wonder and awe are never again so easily lost to him. And so with the artist. If he can touch the life of the people of faith he can know himself as a person, a child of God with a face and a destiny. He will then be able to identify the movements of the spirit in his own life, and to know that his deepest craving is for God, the Creator, whose action is in and through and above all.

Art once had this kind of interdependent association with the church. The church was the origin and stimulus for creative works. Intellect and imagination flourished as an awareness of God pervaded all aspects of the common life. Prophets and artists alike were telling that God had come in Christ, the kingdom of heaven was here and now.

The cold darkness of the catacombs did not silence the news. There, Christian art was born. On the stony expanse of buried walls, artists depicted in symbols and pictures the experience of God's saving power. Many primitive Christians, encouraged and assured as they moved through these torchlit galleries, went out to face the martyrdom of the Roman arena.

When the Christian community could live again in the light of day it built its dwellings into the sky, songs of praise in masonry and stone. In the mosaics and pillars and vaulted ceilings of cathedrals, art found expression for the eternal toward which it reached. Its address to God became an address to the world. The vast numbers who could not read were confronted by the Christ of the paintings. These were the layman's first classes in the Old and New Testaments.

Art suffered in its withdrawal from the Christian influence, and the church lost the gifts of beauty and revelation which the artist brought to its life. It also lost the artist as an evangelist, for art could not speak of that which the artist did not hear and see and handle. Now an impoverished church is beginning to remember that Christ found the Twelve at their work, and that there too we will find the artist.

We envision that within several years the Potter's House Workshop will include a number of groups within the scope of its life.

Through its elementary classes the Workshop hopes always to be in touch with those who have not had a previous creative experience and want to explore the various arts and crafts. The classes will serve in many ways. They will perhaps help some to discover themselves as artists so that they can hear the call to forsake all and follow the vocation of artist. Marjory Bruce* in writing on the development of crafts said that King Edward III passed a law requiring every artificer to choose his "mystery" and having chosen

---

* *The Book of Craftsmen* (London: G. G. Harrup & Co., 1936).

it, practice no other. She tells us that the word "mystery" has completely lost its ancient meaning, and that in the old days it meant a handicraft or art, into the mysteries of which an apprentice had been admitted. She says further that it was a skilled operation, and that the man who chopped wood did not belong to a "mystery," but the man who carved it did. In the ancient meaning of that word the classes will enable gifted persons to choose that mystery into which they would enter.

The classes are also intended for those who may never find in art a primary calling, but who will learn the feel of materials, the joy of shaping them, and who will know through their efforts an appreciation of color, form, and design.

In time there will also be specialized classes for the very young. Perhaps this is a gift the church can make to a technological age. Sir Herbert Read has written:

> An education of the sensibilities—what I have elsewhere called an education through art—is not the present concern of our schools. Something is done at the primary stage—at kindergarten and infant schools; but the child is then quickly swallowed up in a system that ignores the evolution of feeling and provides no time for the free and joyous activity of art. To know becomes the exclusive aim of education: to create is the concern of a tiny minority that evades the social pattern of our technological civilization. The growing child gradually loses all contact with things, all capacity to manipulate materials or discriminate forms. Unless we can discover a method of basing education on these primary biological processes, not only shall we fail to create a society united in love: we shall continue to sink deeper into disunity, mass neuroses and war.*

Perhaps the church can serve this age as it ministers to the young through art, but also as it ministers to the very old who now so often sit in tragic aloneness with nothing to unite them to life. Through its aged alone America could become a nation aware of handicrafts and practiced in their production. Some day we may

---

* *Adventures of the Mind* (New York: Alfred A. Knopf, 1960), pp. 158–159.

discover that a mission of the Workshop is the introduction of crafts to the elderly.

There may also be offered at the Renewal Center classes especially designed for those who are emotionally disturbed and who need the therapy that comes through working with metal, wood, and clay.

Jacqueline Gainsford, who was the first person to be reached by the Workshop, let us see in a concrete way how we can use the odd structure of a Workshop to announce the kingdom of God. When she first came to the church the Workshop was in its exploratory stage, and was gathering literature on the work of other craft centers. We did not guess the part that this research would play in Jacqueline's life until there came a time when she was experiencing great inner turmoil and upheaval, a "shaking of the foundations." She expressed then the need for a time of retreat and we told her of the Penland Craft Center because the literature suggested that it was not only a place of creativity but a place of quiet. At Penland, Jacqueline discovered a dormant love to create with her hands, and to experiment with colors and designs.

After several weeks at Penland, Jacqueline returned to Washington. Soon afterward she told Kay that in a time of prayer it had been revealed to her that it was right to go ahead with craft work and also that it was God's intention to bring into existence a craft center in connection with the church. Kay told her then about the plans for the craft center. She listened in amazement. Up until that time she had known nothing about the Workshop. From then on she was to feel a definite inner sense of mission regarding it. In the next four months she worked on various projects under Kay's direction. These months she later described as "a time of further turmoil and breaking up within. I denied God's love," she said "and had no sense of being loved or accepted within the Church of the Saviour fellowship. Yet I was reaching out for a belonging."

When the Workshop officially began on the third floor of the church, Jacqueline helped Kay prepare test tiles in preparation for the evening classes in enameling. "At last," she wrote, "colors came into the picture. About ten apprentices enrolled in the class and we started with the basics of designs which were drawn and cut out, and with Kay guiding us in constructive criticism on one another's work. All of us protested any creative ability, myself most strongly."

During the next months Jacqueline continued to experiment with color and design, and the technique of firing, while we marveled at the results, but far more wondrous was the work of creation which went on in Jacqueline. Christ became more and more a reality. As she continued to work in the third-floor room, it seemed to her that the Holy Spirit acted to temper her spirit. At times she knew further shaking within, but there invariably followed a deep peace. Kay began to encourage her to work on plaques and to begin using religious symbols. At first she denied any ability to do this, feeling hopelessly inadequate. "I think," she said, "partly due to Kay's encouragement and belief in me, I consented to try. Then I realized my great need of God's help, and began to pray each time I sat down to work, 'Lord, send Thy Holy Spirit upon me, so that whatsoever I do is of Thee.' Often after this I felt a power working through me and a guiding hand at my elbow."

Jacqueline's enamel work is now on sale at both the Potter's House and the Workshop. In color and design it makes a ministry, speaking of the Christ who has become real to her. This is really what structures are all about. They are to help a person find God. The Workshop opens up many possibilities for this, more than one little church shall ever realize. What we have discovered with every task we put our hands to is that one door opens always on another, and that there is no end to what waits to be done. Every once in a while someone will ask Gordon, "If you had it to do over again, would you start the Church of the Saviour?" Most of the time he answers an emphatic "Yes." But sometimes he will say, "No, I think I would like to be the minister of the Potter's House or the Potter's House Workshop making its way in one of the structures of the world." When we ask him why he would want to be limited to one structure when as a member of this church he can be involved in them all, he reviews some of the possibilities inherent in the Workshop. Our finiteness will never permit us to be involved there to the extent that is possible for Kay, who, ordained or not ordained, is the lay minister of this growing congregation. Hers is a ministry limited only by her own sense of destiny and mission and willingness to walk with Him for whom no dream is too vast.

One day while we talked of this, two young ministers who were attending a Baptist convention in Washington dropped by. We shared with them the Workshop's dream of bringing over a European artist who might want the experience of living in America and sharing in the life of the Workshop, or the possibility of having several Christian art students selected by the World Council of Churches to intern at the Workshop. As we discussed these and other exciting possibilities wrapped up in this one project, we asked ourselves aloud why it is we are sometimes guilty of making the Christian faith so colorless and prosaic when it can be the most exciting of all adventures. One minister said, and we think he was right, "It's because it is exciting only when we have the courage to take the risk of following—of getting out beyond the place of safe return."

Those who respond to the instruction and mission of the Workshop will have the opportunity of being apprentices in one of the arts. Apprentices will have the special teaching attention of the staff, who will guide and nurture as well as instruct. It is hoped that in this way apprentices will discover not only the mysteries of an art or handicraft, but the mystery of the Body of Christ: "Lo, I tell you a mystery."

As dedicated persons are led to commit their specific talents wholly to God, the Potter's House Guild will come into being. Together, Guild members will study, pray, explore, and work. Some might discover a special field of mission, such as work with the aged or the young. Others might be engaged wholly in the creation of articles which would be placed on sale at the Workshop and at the coffee house as well as through a mail-order catalogue. Here alone is a tremendous opportunity, for it is almost impossible to find gifts which have spiritual significance that are not sentimental and oftentimes vulgar. Even the lovely hill town of Assisi in Italy has nothing to give its visitors except cheap little medals of St. Francis. Religious items offered in America and Europe are far below the acceptable standards of other items which are not intended to speak of beauty and humility, and of the spirit of God. This simply means that the things of God have to be grasped by more than the mind. Religious items do not just happen because we will them, or because we have an intellectual understanding of a Christian teaching, or because there is a market for "holy" articles. Religious art is always an expression of the incarnate life of Christ in the heart of the craftsman, which through prayer and consecrated work is given form. The artist reveals to others only that which has been revealed to him.

If out of the Workshop can come a little group of people committed to living the common life—to being the twelve together —then God can commission and empower them to take the gospel to the world through the medium of art. No miracle of imagination is needed to envision what these gifted twelve might do.

A miracle is needed nonetheless, but it is the one of conversion that will let an artist with his individual endowment of temperament live in community with fellow artists. Those of us who know how difficult community is with any group of people, know that the problems are not lessened but magnified when a group of artists come together. Persons of the same calling may stimulate one another, but they also more easily threaten one another, and it is soon evident that jealousy, envy, and greed are the enemies within which must be overcome in the trek of the Christian artist. This is true for anyone who follows the vocation of holiness. The artist is fortunate in that the conditions of his life make his problems more apparent. Membership in a Workshop Guild more than membership in most groups makes clear the cost of discipleship, makes the command to die to oneself more obviously a necessity. As the young minister said, do we have the courage to take the risks involved, to share with others the coveted mysteries of our art or craft, to seemingly give up or defer our own little careers to create the modern equivalent of the medieval guild? It will not happen unless God calls a handful of people and gives to them a conviction that through this Guild the winds of God might blow, that here art might take up again its prophetic mission: the divine-human work of creation which always ushers in the new.

13 *What the World Needs*

There were times when Dayspring, the Rockville House Congregation, the Potter's House, and the Workshop seemed far removed from the world in which we lived. Were these defenses against atomic warfare? In the face of the growing possibility of being hurled into the presence of God, did we want these structures to express our life as the Christian community?

We stood sometimes in the candlelight of the Potter's House and watched the people pass in and out, talking of this and that, and never guessing that they were in a house of prayer. Ours was a world in imminent danger of destruction. Were we content that our words to that world await the question, "What must I do to be saved?"

The Sunday sermon interpreted our week, caught up its feelings and undertones, spoke to us where we were so that the Word of God sounded in our lives. Gordon Cosby could proclaim that Word because he lived with us under it, was bound by the same covenant, shared in the life of the community, was subject to its members, upheld by its prayers, asking always, "What would God have me do in this moment?" This was the question beneath the questions, "What does a Christian do in the midst of our kind of world?" "How does he spend his days?" "Is his responsibility different for different hours?"

As nuclear testing was resumed and tension mounted, Gordon preached the sermon that we sometimes call his Doomsday Sermon.

What the World Needs Is Saints

If we are to accept the challenge of the crisis of our times, we, as Christians, must know that the world's deepest need is for saints. These are people who can give themselves in ways which seem fanatical to those who live by the usual ethical and moral norms. These are people who live normally by the second mile. It is not sporadic with them. They have thrown the familiar "duty" maps away. They are utter fools for Christ's sake. They are always finding some cruel little cross to climb up on. They stay there and suffer even when the people deride them and mock them, and thereby they stay closer to Him who stayed on His cross until he died. Now, if Christ be *not* God, they are utter fools, but if Christ be God, then they are the only sane people in the midst of the insane.

These Christians are a people who will throw themselves into the breach between the peace and healing of God and the loneliness, anguish, and terror of the world's lost. They stand as a bridge between man and God, willing, even eager, to become ground grain, broken bread, crushed grapes, poured-out wine. They are willing to be fed upon by the earth's hungry until those hungry ones can feed directly upon Jesus. The world has always needed such people, and it has survived because, here and there, there have been a few such people. But the point now is that the world is not likely longer to survive unless there are many such people—unless you become such a person and unless I become such a person. I do not believe this to be an idle threat. I believe that the human race is in immediate danger of extinction.

There is no need to review the crescendo of terror which we are in. We will not go into the details of that which we are so aware of, although I believe it is important that we be willing to face the imminence and gruesomeness of that which is upon us. Christians, who in the true sense of the word are realists, should be willing to look down into the abyss of disaster into which we are being drawn.

We should be able to face three possibilities. The first is that we shall be among those instantaneously destroyed, along with those whom we are close to—those whom we love. I think this is a real possibility. I think we will live with more freedom and less anxiety if we look at this squarely.

The second possibility we should be able to face is that we shall be among those who are slowly destroyed. This is a more frightening possibility, especially if ones whom we love shall also be among those slowly destroyed.

The third possibility is that we will be of the remnant left for the carrying on of life on this planet. One of the tasks of our church, of the church as a whole, is to prepare us to face one of these possibilities, but especially the third.

Suppose we are one of those chosen to continue the drama of God upon the earth, to pass on the gospel of Jesus Christ, to let future generations know convincingly that Jesus has come to our planet, to build a new civilization out of the ruins? Would we be prepared for this strange honor? This is one of the tasks of our nurturing and training program. When seen in this light one cannot consider our educational schedule too rigorous.

The crisis which is upon us, however, is not to be the primary motivating factor of our lives. There is something phony in saying that we are in imminent danger of losing life itself and all that we hold dear, therefore, let us respond more fully to God's imperative that we may avoid this. As Christians this cannot be what impels us. Suppose the immediate crisis passes, as well it might. If the prayers of millions of people are lifted to God, if these prayers are backed by the lives and costly service of millions of Christians, then the balance can be tipped and our world may be relatively safe from the danger of extinction.

Then what? Well, millions would still be living in anguish and terror. Thousands would still be facing the loneliness of death every day, and the judgment of God. Hospitals would still be crowded with sufferers screaming their pain or bearing it in mute dignity. Men would still be out of work. Children would still be starving to death. A fourth of our city would still be destitute, and thousands sightless. And this is the world whose streets Jesus walks by day and by night.

But suppose there were no sufferers of the sort we are describing —no hungry, no naked, no people in anguish and panic and terror. Every person would still need God, and every person would still be estranged from him until they came to know him through Jesus Christ.

We cannot say that the imperative is the crisis which is upon us. The imperative is not the world's hungry. There was no possibility of a doomsday bomb when Jesus died, nor when a few weeks later a band of God-intoxicated, Holy Spirit-filled men and women spilled out of that upper room to fill the breach between the peace and healing of God and the loneliness and terror of Jerusalem's lost. The imperative for them was that they had been grasped by God.

They had found what it was to be real persons in community. They had discovered that to be alive at all was to be pouring out their lives, to be breaking the alabaster jar of their lives as their Master did on his cross. They had to do this because they belonged to Him, not in order to save the world from destruction. As a by-product, they were the world's salt and life.

We also have been grasped by God. We've met Him on His cross. We've met Him in His living resurrection power. What can we do? Not to save the world from destruction, although the stakes are unbelievably high. What can we do?

Anything which we do as a church and anything we do publicly in our city, first of all, will grow out of an inward awareness and holiness. It is fundamental to everything which we do as Christians, that we personally develop a style of life which is recognizably Christian. This means that in our family groups, in our businesses and our government offices, when we walk in, a light goes on. This style of life will be recognizable in all of our personal contacts with public servants in transportation, mail, laundry, and milk; with servicemen, salesmen, telephone operators, trash collectors, janitors, hospital attendants, elevator operators—to anyone who serves us in any way. We shall mediate something to every person we meet.

We will take with terrible seriousness the sins which plague us: gluttony, sloth, lust, avarice, envy, jealousy, and pride. We will not trifle with these things. It's amazing to me how often we think in terms of a vocation, a public corporate vocation, when our lives are morally confused and bewildered, and we have not cleaned up the very basic things which have to do with personal morality. The New Testament makes it very plain that we have to deal with this. There will be a simple honesty, openness, a transparency about us; an honesty when we are alone filling out our income tax form, and making sure that when we take sick leave we are sick. We will pay our bills. When we borrow money, we will return it. When we say we will do something, we do it.

We will know something of repentance. I increasingly have the feeling that more cleansing and more healing can come to our world through repentance than any other way. In the words of the publican, "God be merciful to me a sinner," or as Jesus put it, "Blessed are they who mourn." The word for mourn is *penthein*. Barclay reminds us: It is the word which the Greeks used in mourning for their dead. It is the word used to describe David's grief for his son, "O Absalom, my son Absalom." It is the grief which comes from a heart which is broken, and the Christian has not gotten started until he knows something about mourning for his sin as one mourns for the departed beloved dead. The realization that we are offenders against the Holy One is very rare. Mistaken? Yes. Foolish? Yes. In error? Yes. But guilty of sin—offenders against a holy God? We are not that. A sense of personal responsibility is hard to find, and repentance is this. It is the realization of guilt before God. This is the reason our modern age does not like the word "sin." It implies personal responsibility. Responsibility for the kind of people we are, the city and the country and the world we live in. If we do not feel our own sin and we do not feel we are to blame corporately, we are not very close to Him because when we are close to Him we know that we are miserable offenders.

We need to know something about repentance and we need to

know about forgiveness. Forgiveness is not that which we extend to a few people, but to all people. One difference between the so-called good Christian and the saint is that the good Christian extends forgiveness to many people, maybe even to most people, but the saint extends forgiveness to all people. What I am saying is that the time is now here when we must forgive those whom we have had difficulty getting along with, those who threaten us and those who hurt us. In the name of Christ we must learn to extend forgiveness even if we die in the process. We cannot be agents of God's reconciliation for the world if we can't handle forgiveness within our own home and within our own neighborhoods, and within our own community of faith.

Now all of this has to do with a hidden holiness. It has to do with the development of a style of life which will be recognizably Christian, so that everywhere we go the people whom we touch will know Christ to a degree.

This in itself, however, is not enough. I am assuming that whatever we do, we do as a part of a community of which Christ is head. Isolated goodness is futile. Every man, to be sure, must be a good Samaritan whenever the occasion arises, but good-Samaritan acts are not adequate now—not in our kind of world. And they never were really adequate in the sort of world which we have known. Whatever we do we must do in a representative capacity. When we go to our work day by day we go as a representative of the people of God, and whatever we do we do in this representative capacity. We are seeking to bring people into the Christian community and not just to affect them individually, but to bring them into the Christian community which can mature them and bring them to the point of ministry; so that their belonging to the people of God takes precedence over every other loyalty, over every other group in which there is a belonging. This is how our own time is to be spent, being the channel of God's grace to bring into being a corporate existence so that people can see the gospel concretized, so that they can see the incarnation actually embodied at some place in time and space. To this we must give our days and our nights.

With Christians everywhere we need to throw away the maps which we have used in the past, to know that we have capacities that we have not exercised. What happens to people under the stimulation of the Holy Spirit is that they discover that they have been living far beneath that of which they are capable. This is the experience of a nation in time of war. It lives on one basis until war is declared and then it lives on another basis altogether. The forty-hour week goes all to pieces and the nation works whatever period it needs to work in order to produce the armaments and tools which are needed to fight a war. A family under financial pressure oftentimes changes its plans. The wife goes to work, the husband works two jobs. A man who is getting established in his business feels that the nine-to-five day is completely foolish. He works the hours which are necessary to get his business established. A professional man such as a doctor works all hours of the day and night because he is dedicated to the care of the sick and he cannot refuse the call for help. What all of this means to you and me is that we have a capacity for greater production. Most of us could do considerably more than we do. We do not need as much time left over for pampering as we get. Most of us do not need as much time for sleep and for recreation and for personal activities. We do not need as much time for those things which we feel we have a right to.

We must make the decision that we will live on a crisis basis because this is the condition in which our world finds itself and this is what the love of God demands anyway. It is just more easily seen in the kind of world in which we shall live out our lives. We are going to do this not for the next week, or the next month—we are going to live on this crisis basis for the rest of our days. We are not going to ask for concessions; we are not going to retire. Sixty-five is a figure we can forget, if we make it to sixty-five. Let us make the decision and then find out if we die of the strain. Now, not many people die of this sort of strain. They die of conflict, they die of pressure and tension. They work too hard because of anxiety, and for them work is an escape though it appears that work has killed a dedicated man. Not too many people who have a quiet center die because they work too hard. When we try it, then we will see whether or not we die and if we do, it won't be too serious. It won't be the first time someone died. It might be a very glorious thing if we died this way, but it may be that we will discover that we are strengthened and as Fosdick says, grace is granted "for the living of these days."

I would make several suggestions. We might take an extra part-time job and give all the proceeds of that extra job to some venture which, in our judgment, will really make a difference.

If we would like to channel the resources of our lives directly, we might give one night a week to some effort for human better-ment, such as the Renewal Center, the Potter's House, or work among the poor, or whatever it happens to be that each of us is doing. If in our mission groups we could think in terms of a second night, this means that an army of trained people would be released. Instead of sixty people to man the Potter's House each week, we would need only thirty, and thirty would be released to work with the city's indigent. Twenty-five per cent of the people in our city are indigent, and the question is, do we really care?

The tragic thing is that very few people ever get past the point of looking after their own situation, their own personal lives and their own families and they keep arguing, "If we take time away from this thing which we need to be working at, if we take it away from our family, we're neglecting this responsibility." This is right at one level and wrong at another level. Unless some peo-ple have time left over, unless they have some love left over, unless they have some resources left over for the people who don't eat, for the people who are desperate, none of us is going to have any family. We are not going to exist at all. It is just that simple. This is what the prophets of God are talking about. We simply cannot live alone.

Our time belongs to God and I think He is not going to give us too much personal time, because there is work to be done. I am not thinking only of the usual sort of work. One of the most costly works and one of the ones which is most urgent for us is the work of intercession. Perhaps some of us could take that second night in solitude for the work of intercession. Suppose when the Rockville House met in the suburbs where it is hard for Christ to get into the lives of His people that there were an equal number of us who spent that time praying that the Holy Spirit would descend and that little house congregation would be so empowered that the people in the neighborhood would want to be a part of the Christian community. Suppose when each of the groups is meeting at the Potter's House that three or four people beginning at seven o'clock would pray and intercede until twelve-thirty. Suppose we were called to that sort of work, thus channeling the Holy Spirit; pleading that He grapple with these people who come; that they might really hear the gospel.

If we would intercede in this way perhaps many who come to the Potter's House would themselves have their own deep spiritual hungers uncovered, would hear the good news in Christ, would themselves become its proclaimers to the poor. We need desperately people called to the ministry of intercession.

Or perhaps we might ask the church where it needs us to be and we might go to school on that second night and get the training that will equip us to be in the places where we are needed.

As a church we need to expand our output. We need to begin to move like a mighty army with banners unfurled. For us moving like a mighty army means a new commitment to the sacrifice of quiet service. It means a people gladly bearing a cross. This is not especially dramatic unless we can see into the inwardness of it.

The little band of disciples came back to Jesus, and all that they had done was to go into the homes of people and talk to them about the good news of Christ, the richness of their faith. And when they came back Jesus said, "I saw you. I saw what was happening. Satan fell like lightning from the sky." This is the drama, but it is the drama of quiet suffering and quiet serving. This is the way the church moves.

I have talked of some of the things we can do. The question is as we wait in the presence of God, what is He calling you to do?

What is your call? What is your mission unto Him? How ought you to go to work. How can you make your life a concrete expression of ground grain, broken bread, crushed grapes, poured-out wine? Ask God how this can become real for you.

*   *   *

There are certain hours which give a new heart and a new spirit. They are hours when the veil between the spiritual and the material world seems to be rent and one knows that if all of life could be lived on the basis of what is seen in those moments, it would be closer to what God intended. They are the times when we hear a Doomsday Sermon and know that the things which make for peace are Renewal Centers and Workshops and the Word made flesh in our coming and going. They are the moments when we see a picture of a starving child in a distant country and know that we cannot live our days as we have lived them; or when we read a book and have the horizons of our little world pushed back. They are the times when we look into the heart of a friend and find him acceptable though he is unacceptable and God lets us see in him every man.

They are the times of reality in which to make commitment—a commitment which will be lived out in the valleys, over long dry stretches when the vision is gone, but the memory alive nonetheless.

Woe unto us if the mountaintop moments find us saying, "I don't want to be carried away by enthusiasm." "I'll wait until I have more perspective." "I'm not the type to follow through," or "I must have time to assess my needs and determine the practical response." In our church we even sometimes say, "I will pray about this" when we mean "I will defer the hour of decision until I am not up against that which in this hour compels me to say 'Yes.' "

Woe unto us if we think that commitment to the moment of vision binds and restricts and keeps us from our destiny. Woe . . . because we roll the stones upon our own tombs, for by night even the most inspired sermon is difficult to remember and by Tuesday it is forgotten, and the casings of self are a little harder and the bonds of the old a little tighter. Great fears and small concerns become the order of the day and it is not recalled that life was to be lived in a different way and that there was a moment in which we were face to face with reality. The decision is never postponed. It is either made or not made in the moment, and always the hour of worship is the hour of commitment.

Christ in the City

There was a wandering clown who visited our city. His name was Pathetique and he came to give laughter to hurt and deprived children. A reporter asked him why children love a clown and he said, "He's a mirror of themselves. He comes as a strange creature from another world and at first the children are a bit frightened. But then he goofs. He tries to fly and fails. And the child says, 'That's me and all the mistakes I make.' "

Pathetique's real name is Larry Evers. He calls on children in orphanages, and hospitals, and settlement houses. The newspaper story says:

Seven years ago, Evers became dissatisfied with his theatrical career. He first turned to religious and social work, but then realized that he could reach children best when he met them as a clown.

He supports himself by doing a little jig on busy street corners and handing out donated flowers. Hotels usually give him complimentary status. He's at the Statler here. Pathetique has no publicity man, secretary, or office. He seeks no paid bookings but says he prefers to wander through the land calling on children "whose poverty is a symbol of their abandonment to God's mercy."

We called Pathetique at the Statler, but he had left and there was no forwarding address. We wanted to talk to him about mission, and we wanted to get to know him because Pathetique,

himself, is abandoned to God's mercy and we felt sure that he
would have something to say to us about vocation and the following of visions.

Pathetique has no certain place to lay his head. He reminds us
that somewhere for someone this quality of abandonment is involved for any mission to get off the ground. The old economic
structures he was caught in did not let him use his talents to be a
person on mission, and he had the kind of spirit which could give
them up in order to find those structures that would. There is
hardly a person who comes into the membership of this church
who does not look at his job with troubled gaze, for he has learned
that in his work the "ministry of the laity" must be lived out, and
so many times our little jobs seem like poor rooftops for proclaim-
ing the news which has been whispered to us in secret. Like
Pathetique, we feel dissatisfied.

Gordon says at this point that either one of two things is true:
"Your dissatisfaction is God's instruction to learn to do every task
to His glory, or it is God calling you to cast your nets in another
place. If it is the first, there will be the contentment of consecrated
work; if it is the latter, the dissatisfaction will persist."

For many the dissatisfaction was lasting. It did not seem to them
that their present jobs were the best structures for their ministries.
Bill Gipson was one of these. He was certain that God was calling
him and those he talked to, to something new and he was certain
that the vocational structures they were seeking should be an
extension of the church, embodying the concept of *koinonia*. The
natural step was to think in terms of Christian businesses, and then
in exploring how they might be launched in terms of a business association. Night after night at the Potter's House and in
special meetings we have met in formal and informal gatherings
to talk about the future of this project. It still has no name and
we refer to it simply as the Association. Its purposes have been
broadly defined as these:

1. *Assessment of ideas.* To assess carefully the merits of ideas
originating from within the Association or received from outside
which might develop into Christian enterprises.

2. *Establish new businesses.* To assist in all possible ways the establishment of new, Christian, privately or corporately owned enterprises, which will become members or associate members of the Association.

3. *Spiritual support.* To provide a fellowship of prayer and study for representatives of member businesses in order that the Holy Spirit might move in them and there be a spirit of oneness in a common venture.

4. *Business support.* To meet together in business sessions for creative thinking and meditation, realizing that the group exists for a kingdom service and that ideas on management, sales programs, etc., will emerge as we wait, listen, pray, and meditate together.

Having articulated its purpose, the next step was to anticipate what God's will might be for these businesses: How were they to be vehicles for the preaching of the gospel? Our thoughts have turned to the depressed areas of Washington, for there the need is obvious and there for a long time we have felt God wants us to be. We have worked with the poor through established agencies, but it is part of our life which we know has to be strengthened, for we know that Christ is concerned with the poor and that the church which lives will be concerned with the poor.

When Evelyn Underhill was an established religious writer and spiritual leader and counselor, that great director of souls, Baron Von Hügel, instructed her to become directly involved with the poor:

I believe you ought to get yourself, gently and gradually, interested *in the poor;* that you should visit them, very quietly and unostentatiously, with as little incorporation as possible into Visiting Societies, etc. You badly want deintellectualizing, or at least developing homely, human sense and spirit dispositions and activities. Gradually you may be able to draw out, perhaps even to help some of these poor religiously. But the good *you yourself* will gain, long before this, and quite apart from this, will be very great. For it will, if properly entered into and persevered with, discipline, mortify, soften, deepen, and quiet you. . . . I would carefully give the preference to the two weekly visitations of the poor against everything else.*

For our good we need the same direct involvement, but such a mission must also have another end if it is to have any power to save. The gospel love does not permit the emphasis to be on our own gain, though it follows that he who loses his life finds it.

We need Pathetiques and Schweitzers who love and care enough to take their one and ten talents and fling them away in the stench and misery of our urban jungles and let those who live there know that there is a resurrection power which can break into their lives and change them.

We have no illusions about the inner city in which our poor live out their days. It is a violent city stalked by street gangs that cannot be controlled, but themselves control the uneducated teeming life of these ghetto jungles. It is a city abandoned by the middle-income white families who have fled to suburbia. Negroes are not permitted to follow, but the churches can follow and many have, leaving the city with all its sin and need. It is a city that the church must take on again through a massive attack, which is to say, through a massive sharing of its life.

It does not seem to us far-fetched that a business association and the businesses it would bring into existence might be the framework for this massive penetration. Already we have one representative of the church in this inner city and she is there because of the Christian business, which is the Potter's House. We met Gladys Stergiou first when the city employment agency sent her in response to a request for cleaning help we needed one summer when Lizzie was on vacation. Gladys was quick and intelligent and eager, and we responded to her and she responded to us. When we could afford someone on a full-time basis to make the various, exotic coffees at the Potter's House we employed Gladys. This was a needful step for we were in difficulty with our coffees. Too many

---

* Margaret Cropper, *The Life of Evelyn Underhill* (New York: Harper & Brothers, 1958), p. 75.

of our coffeemakers were of that school that scorn recipes and add a dash of something here and a bit of something there. A customer would say, "I want my Turkish coffee just the way you made it last night," and we would have to confess that we did not know how it was made last night or how it would be made tomorrow night.

Gladys put an end to this problem and became a member of the working team on every night and of the study-and-prayer group on Thursday night. Her home is the inner city. She has been to high school but she also has been to the school of pickpockets. Next to her home is a house of prostitution. Gambling and bootlegging are among other thriving businesses in her block. There is no lack of schools in the neighborhood. One can learn yoking, how to cut dope (take it), and make dummy paper (counterfeit). Gladys knows how to make a living in this world and she turned from it slowly as she glimpsed through the coffee house not only a people that was different, but a people that she wanted to belong to and one that would accept her.

"The first time I noticed that you were different," she says, "was in the way you entertained in a party you gave at the coffee house. No one was loud and there was no vulgar language. The men did not molest the women and there was no drinking, and still everyone was having fun. I had more fun than I had experienced since I was a kid. And then, you all went home at a decent hour. Our parties start at eleven or twelve o'clock and are over at dawn."

Gladys didn't come to church for a long time. She explained this by saying, "Eighty-five per cent of the people I know go to church in the morning and back to their bootlegging in the afternoon, but they go in order to have a big funeral when they die."

The first time Gladys came to church was on Christmas day, 1960. The chapel was filled to overflowing and she and her ten-year-old son were seated in the hall. "Throughout the service we smiled at each other. We thought it funny to be sitting in the hall, and for there to be no shouts and no Amens." Gladys let us see how strange we sometimes look to others and how closely we are sometimes watched.

As we think of a spearhead into the inner city it seems to us that Gladys' experience is significant. One by one pieces of dreams seem to come together. We have decided that the ministry of our Christian businesses will be to an underprivileged area and that we will think not only in terms of businesses which express the mission of the church, but businesses which are related to the needs of the poor. We have long thought of a factory with a product adapted to unskilled labor. Once we had thought of its being at Dayspring and providing employment for the aged or handicapped. We had talked then of its profits going to a mission in a foreign country. Now we begin to see this factory, not a large one, in a depressed area of the city. It might employ only four or eight people on an assembly-line product, which could be the creation of the Workshop and change from month to month. It might even be a ceramic factory with the Workshop producing the designs and molds. The factory would be open at night so that we might volunteer our work there on the same basis as we do at the Potter's House. Not only would this enable the workers to have larger salaries than unskilled labor brings, but it would enable us to be in relationship with them. It would not be a totally unequal situation because many of our people from time to time need this kind of job, nor would the work be limited to unskilled labor. There would have to be sound management, sales, and distribution of commodities produced. This would mean additional, meaningful employment for committed sales and executive personnel. Always at the heart of the factory would be relationship. We would dare speak to these people about Him whom we love as we dared to become involved in the structures which involved them—to serve them and to be served by them.

The factory would give any profits to the Association, while other Christian businesses would simply tithe to the Association. The Association would use its funds to bring into existence other Christian businesses or improved housing or service projects. Each Christian business as it grew would attempt to employ people from the area with all the difficulties inherent for the person who must make the transition from relief or other means of sustenance to the dignity of self-support. One of the essential services would be a day nursery, for so often fathers are not in evidence and the mother must be the wage-earner if the family is not eligible for relief.

As we batted this idea back and forth it took on new dimensions. A doctor and a lawyer in our fellowship said that they would like to offer their services. This made us begin to think in terms of an old warehouse or other dwelling which could be converted into an Association building that might house some of the businesses as well as provide office space for the Christian doctor, dentist, lawyer, psychologist, teacher, and minister. There would be need for anyone who had a skill and wanted to offer his services not only to transform a blighted area but to give to its people a hope of glory. If other churches wanted to share, it could be an ecumenical adventure and could provide the massive attack which is necessary.

The plan now is that the Association will establish itself with the issuing of stock. The stock would be available to anyone who wanted to share in the adventure. The purchasers would be nonvoting members of the Association, while the voting members would be the representatives of these businesses which are located in a specific depressed area for the purpose of the renewal of that area.

What are the ways in which the Association is getting under way? One is a Professional Art Rental Service with a threefold purpose:

1. To incorporate into the existing decor of an office or reception room a creative atmosphere by bringing to the attention of clients and visitors the works of leading Washington artists.

2. To make the hours that clients spend waiting for appointments or conferences more pleasing.

3. To provide gallery space for Washington's many competent artists, thereby providing a link between the artist and his community.

Barbie Longfellow launched this business without a cent, but with the willing help of those who felt called to be a part of the

Association. Bill Gipson repositioned the desk in his own one-man office in order that Barbie could move her desk in and have a business address and telephone. The paintings were made available by Washington artists who hoped to widen their following and to sell their paintings. Ralph Talbot took colored slides of each picture so that prospective customers could know what was available.

It took more capital to launch the second enterprise, which is an offset printing press. Stock was issued in the amount of $6,000. There were two classes available: nonvoting stock B which was offered to any interested friend, and voting stock A which was available only to church members. A large part of the capital was used in the purchase of equipment. Its small beginning was again on the third floor of our church. When quarters were found for the Workshop, the Potter's Press moved in with it. In addition to the handling of strictly commercial orders, it prints all the literature as well as cards and the artistic creations of the Workshop.

The press is Peg Gummere's first experience with printing. A few elementary lessons came with the equipment, but they were hardly sufficient to launch a printing business in a highly competitive field. However, at crucial moments God has provided. When she was struggling with her first letterhead job and about to despair, a man who had been twenty years a multilith operator caught a glimpse of the new equipment from the street. When he leaned down for a better look into the basement room he was amazed to discover that a woman was the operator. On further observation he saw that she was in trouble. Five minutes later he was hard at work and four hours later they together completed the job.

The economic foothold of the Potter's Press is not yet secure, but we are hopeful about its survival. Again, it is a project with unlimited potential for mission. Like every other project it is intertwined with the work of other missions though this was not the intention. The press prints the literature which every mission needs. The Workshop helps the press with designs for attractive brochures and mailing pieces and will create the products for the factory when it comes into existence, as well as offering therapy classes for the Renewal Center. The Potter's House channels students into the

Workshop classes, while the Renewal Center will provide the trained psychiatric personnel which will aid in the rehabilitation of those in the depressed area. Dayspring gives to each mission opportunity for the deepening of its life in Christ in order that these various missions may express the one mission of the Church. Here in miniature is a glimpse of the interdependence of the church everywhere and that upbuilding in love and bodily growth which occur when each part is working properly.

Other businesses will probably get underway this next year. Some may fail, but each one will have made some little contribution; it will not be black failure, but failure with the hope of God in it.

How does a mission start? In small ways as God speaks to one person and then to another. Wally Wilson, who was brought up in an orphanage, pondered the mission to the depressed areas and said to Gordon one day,

"If I could learn, I think I would like to offer my services to cut hair in the depressed areas."

It so happens that Gordon's barber runs a barber school. When he told Pete that Wally was a white-collar member of his church who wanted to cut hair in order to be on mission to the poor of the city, Pete waived the $300 tuition charge and gave Wally his barber tools at cost. So every weekday night and all day Saturday Wally goes to barber school. Pete says Wally has a real feel for cutting hair, but it is still going to take him a thousand hours to get his certificate.

Out yonder lies an Association, but we respond to it in this moment in what we see and know to do now. And there is Gladys, and Wally, and Zosima to illustrate the mission and the way.

Zosima is a small, pretty Filipino woman. When we met her first she was living in one of the worst slum areas of Washington with her husband and seven bright-eyed children who seemed as yet untouched by the misery around them. Thelma Rutherford, a member of our church, was the family's social worker. She had put Zosima in touch with Dorothy Cresswell, who with several other church members was leading a study-and-prayer project in Zosima's neighborhood.

When it was the time of our annual Christmas party we needed someone to serve in the kitchen with Lizzie, and Thelma told us that Zosima needed the money and that we could count on her to be there.

The party was just getting started in a fairyland setting of silver and gold when Zosima arrived. Gordon greeted her at the door and from then on she was passed warmly from person to person with the brief explanation that she was from the Southwest Project, which everyone knew to be the area where a little mission group was engaged. When Dorothy arrived several hours later she was surprised and delighted to see Zosima and whisked her off to the second floor where there was more food and more punch and lights and "beautiful people."

While all this went on poor Lizzie issued loud complaints from the kitchen. Our small efforts did not compensate for the help that had not arrived. When we finally discovered that Zosima was that help, we reluctantly brought her the news that she was needed by Lizzie. To make up for it we kept dropping in on her and generally assisting.

Thelma told us later that when Zosima got home that night, she was so excited that she woke her husband and all the children and with sweets left from the night had a Christmas party for them, while she said over and over, "They really wanted me!"

This is all that we hope to do: to build the structures which will give the poor of our city the spirit of a party that they may come to know Him who can change their lives, that they may come to know that love is real and that they are wanted.

15 *Toward a New Land*

The brownstone house that has held so much of our life together has on the small brass plaque to the left of its door strangely prophetic words: Headquarters of the Church of the Saviour. Those who placed that sign there understand better today what it means, for the church is beginning to exist in a Workshop, in a Renewal Center, in a printing press, and in a coffee house.

Sometimes when the fire of faith burns low and we forget that the Maker and Builder is God we look at the structures of the Church of the Saviour and anxious thoughts come. It seems then that we move too fast and that there are too few of us, and that we are in too many places, and that we are too inadequate for the tasks which we have taken up. In such a moment someone said to Gordon,

"Can't you see the weaknesses everywhere and the possibility that all these little structures we are building are going to come tumbling down?"

"That which is in God cannot be shaken," he replied. "If it is not of God, then let us praise Him when it collapses so that we can get on with the next thing, because surely we don't want to give our lives to building what is not His will."

We assured him that it was not structures which concerned us but the people who had given day in and day out at unbelievable cost to make them possible.

"What about them?" we asked. "It is their hurt that matters."

"That in them which is of Christ," he said, "cannot be shaken. And that which is not, they will want to let go. The structures are not important. It is what happens to us and everyone who will be involved in them which is important."

We learned again and in another way that we did not exist to serve the structures, but they existed to serve us. We had set in the public eye a coffee house and for some of us it came above all other things—and we had good spiritual reasons, for we had said it belonged to God and named it the Potter's House, and dedicated our nights there to Him. We had articulated for one another the Law of the Potter's House, the Rule by which we would live; a holy rule it was, for it would enable us to channel the life of the church to the world. But all laws are schoolmasters to draw us closer to Christ. It is difficult to get that forever straight. Time and again the sleeping Pharisee, the standardbearer in each one, rose up to flay us with harsh words and make us judges over our brothers. It all seemed right because Christ's work was at stake, the witness of His Church. Then out of the community came a voice to say again that the structures were not important. It was the same voice that was forever telling us how important they were. We understood nonetheless, and had anew the discovery that we were not made for the sabbath, but the sabbath for us.

The conversation on structures more than any other helped some of us to free others to do the impossible, and to free them to bear their own burdens. We often have the temptation of the professional to want to rush in and to somehow hold everything together. It is easy to see why we have kept going in our churches those things which should have been allowed to die natural or unnatural deaths. We keep propping up that which should be recognized for the disaster it is so that it can either receive transfusions of new life, or be allowed to expire, in which case we can face our sin and know that we are forgiven and face our inadequacy and know that we are acceptable.

For the church is God's church and He watches over it, and there is a sense in which we who love that church need never be anxious for it. This is hard to grasp because there is another sense in which it is dependent upon us, and our response is the only all-important thing.

In our little fellowship it is our response which has sometimes made us fearful for the structures which hold and nurture our life together. On the way to building them, we have often stopped to discuss with one another who was the greatest, in the subtle and not-so-subtle ways that knowledgeable people do. We know why Christ said so many times, "Whoever would be great among you must be your servant, and whoever would be first among you must be slave of all." We forever find ourselves seeking the highest place at the table. There is a glorious sense in which we are bound to one another under the lordship of Christ, and a terrible sense in which we have known under this lordship all the problems of the Twelve together.

There is a myth which has grown up around the Church of the Saviour so that visitors who linger with us long are surprised to find how very human is the *koinonia* here. Part of the rumor is that we have grown beyond being divided by ego needs. They say that the Church of the Saviour has an unusual amount of artistic talent, as can be seen in its building and crafts and paintings; they have wealthy members, as is evidenced by their budget; they are intellectuals, as is evidenced by their reading and membership requirements; and they have a lot of energy and emotional health, which their varied activities bear witness to. In addition to this, they all talk well. They have the gift of communication.

If all this were true, we know not what message the church would find in it. But as it is, our most creative people came to us unaware of their creative gifts. They help explode the theory that only the minority can create. Sadly enough, almost all of us in this fellowship come out five dollars short each month instead of five dollars ahead. Economics is one of the sources of pressure and strain which we know. It is out of poverty that we have so often given. As for intellectuals, we are not intellectual enough to know if we have them or not. Our guess is that we do not. We have some Great Books clubs which meet at the coffee house, and they give us the impression of being benevolently tolerant of our limitations in this regard. As for our growth in the spirit, we seem so many times like infants "needing to be fed with milk." Our relationships here and there are plagued by lack of trust in one another, by wounds that have not healed, by insecurities, by the self which wants to establish its own kingdom. We are destined never to grow beyond this, for even if the seventy who are now members could move as a body on to the next level of the spiritual spiral, as a membership we would not have made it, because always new people are coming in and they have to start where everyone begins. But even for the old, the thorn in the flesh is sometimes a relationship that is not healed. Surely this is not the way God intends it, but it serves its redemptive purpose for it keeps us more conscious of our dependence on Him and our need to grow in the life of prayer. Then God has a way of redeeming one part of us and bringing another unredeemed part into view, so that even that modern saint, Evelyn Underhill, said in middle years, "At bottom I'm unchristian still."

Sometimes we have looked at the sins of this fellowship and wondered what makes us different from groups which do not know Christ as Lord, and the answer is always, "Commitment," a commitment which makes us willing to live in the tension of unresolved relationships. However long it takes, however much it costs, we are committed to bridging any gulf which divides us from another. We exist under the lordship of One who says in the cross of Calvary that this is the way.

We exist under the lordship of One who took a towel and a basin and told us to do likewise. Our commitment is to overcoming that which keeps us from being lowly and meek in heart. In some of our thoughts and words and actions we may clamor for the high place but we have a commitment that ever intrudes to remind us that we are to be enablers of one another. We know that to abide in the truth of the New Testament, we simply have to be a serving people. We have to overcome that in ourselves which keeps our groups from taking the form of the suffering servant.

We do not have to be successful according to what the world

calls success. Our ministry is not secured because we succeed. Jesus Christ is our security. We do not have to raise our standard of living to whatever the next level may be. We simply have to serve. This is how you get to belong to this odd assortment of people and to the Lord of this people. Those terrible words "purgation" and "interior crucifixion" are all part of it, for there is always a self that wants to be served rather than to serve. We keep learning this in our mission groups. We find it a good, warm feeling to serve, to be needed, but this is provided that we can do it on our own terms. There are many things which we do if we choose to do them, but to be given the opportunity to serve when we had not planned on it so often gives us the feeling, "Who are these people getting in our way?"

This call to which we have made response is a call to die to self, but to die in order that we may belong to Him who issues the call and to those who make similar response. This is what heaven is all about. This is what makes beautiful the words "purgation" and "crucifixion." They give us a Lord and a people, "Once you were no people but now you are God's people." For all its spots and wrinkles and creases, this fellowship is touched by a grace. To belong to it is to have a Person to belong to, to have a people with whom one's life is forever mysteriously bound. It is to have the deep hungers of the heart satisfied. It is to be given a vision which breaks the limitations of one's little life. It is to know from whence we come and whither we go, and what is the work of our days. It is to be rich though poor. It is to be free though bound.

Jesus breathed on His disciples and said, "Receive the Holy Spirit." This is the covering which is laid over all sin. "Love covereth a multitude of sins."

We need ever to be intercessors for one another and intercessors for our groups that we may be open to the receiving of this gift of the Holy Spirit, and something can break in our lives and in the lives of our mission groups and they can be channels of His power. Intercessory prayer is not a new discovery, but it is the most important rediscovery of the church in our time. We stand on the threshold of a New Reformation, but it will not come except as we are intercessors, congregations which gather to pray, to look into the face of Christ and to give praise. There will be no revival, renewal, or rebirth without worshiping, praying congregations. This is the mainspring of the Ecumenical Movement, for here we discover our oneness as a congregation and our oneness as the church of Christ in the world. We become ecumenical as we enter into depth commitment and as we deepen the life of worship and adoration. The church is not organized into unity. The merger takes place in mind and heart and spirit as a people gathers and the Holy Spirit is given as it was at Pentecost. It is then that we are empowered to take a gospel to the world. Again we do not try to unite in order that we can be on mission, but it is as we are on mission that we move into the unity which has been given us in Jesus Christ.

This is our experience with the coffee house. It was not the world which responded to the first news story, but the church—the church in Kansas and Ohio and New York and Iowa and Nebraska, and Colorado and the church in far lands. A minister in Edinburgh, Scotland, wrote, "It was rather a coincidence that I overheard a conversation during lunch at New College here in Edinburgh which made me perk up my ears. It concerned a coffee house to be opened by the people of your parish." The church responded by its prayers, its contributions, and its good wishes, and we knew in a deeper way than we had ever known before that we belonged to this church spread out in time and space. Any grace falling on part of it affected the whole. We were members one of another. Every member belonged to every other member. We shared in the health of the whole and we shared in the sickness of the whole.

Again, when the coffee house opened we were in dialogue with the church in a way that had never happened before. We had gone to the market place to be with the world, but the church goes there to talk to us about mission because there the church is on mission. The leaders of Christendom have picked up trays and waited tables, and in between customers we have shared our dreams and hopes and plans. Around our coffee tables we have talked together on what should be the strategy of the Christian army, and we have known a burning of our hearts within and looking back we have known that Another joined us.

This is what has happened at every mission point. It happened with the Workshop and now it is happening with the Association as we plan and dream about how we can move down into a depressed area of our city. It becomes clear to us that we cannot do it alone, but a person from this church and a person from that church says, "I want to help," and it seems possible. There is no kind of service not needed in these areas: medical, legal, various sorts of teaching of the arts and music, counseling, many other skills. The Association can be a structure which can make it possible for literally hundreds of Christians—Roman Catholics and Baptists and Episcopalians and Church of God—to converge upon a city and lift it into the light of God. The chapel in the Association Building can be and must be an ecumenical chapel where the church of Washington worships in order that it might be empowered to take the gospel to the poor. We cannot go as "do-gooders" in this city. The Scriptures warn us against going at all until we are sent:

> I did not send the prophets,
>   yet they ran;
> I did not speak to them,
>   yet they prophesied.
> But if they had stood in my council,
>   then they would have proclaimed
>   my words to my people.
>
> Jeremiah 23:21-22

As we begin to penetrate in our mission the darkness of the world in a way which is costly enough, in a way which is dangerous enough, we will begin to be aware of our unity which has been given us. This may be the way that we will discover that we belong to one another. When you share a common danger and a common risk, there is a fusion of life.

We look at our coffee house, and our Workshop, and dreams too many to utter, and we know that it is not intended that we do it all. Each church must have a dynamic thrust into its environs so that the church again becomes a serving people and membership is on the basis of where a person is called under Christ to serve.

The age of world missions as we have known it is over. Each church now has a missionary task for its direct environment. Bishop Lesslie Newbigin of the Church of South India told the Third Assembly of the World Council of Churches meeting in New Delhi that he hoped "the churchmen of Asia and Africa, having studied the spiritual situation of some of the older churches, will be moved to send missionaries to Europe and America to make the Gospel credible to the pagan masses of these continents who remain unmoved by the witness of the churches in their midst." Those are words to ponder, for they help us begin to see that the missionary task is now primarily around our existing churches whether these churches be in the East or in the West. This does not mean that we forget the "ends of the earth." We need to make concrete our belonging to the church in other lands, and we do this when we share concretely in her task. We do not belong to the church in Washington, D. C., or to the church in America, or to the church in Africa. We belong to the church in the world. Last year the little country of Ceylon sent $1,000 to the East Harlem Protestant Parish in New York City. In Ceylon $1,000 is comparable to $10,000 in America. It would have been easy for the church there to have looked at this parish set in the midst of a rich country and said, "Let them get it from some place there." To work only in our own situation would be to distort mission, but to see mission only in terms of other countries is to have a new age out of focus.

In our small fellowship we have talked much about taking a city for Christ, but this is oratory if we think we are to do it alone. This city will become Christ's when the church in Washington becomes a serving people and to belong to that church is to be part of a fellowship that serves. We have a few ways in which we seek to serve this city, but we touch only a small segment of the need. There is hospital work to do and prison work. There is work with the aged and work with the young who are healthy and those who are sick and those who are juvenile delinquents. We need exciting structures which will grapple realistically with local issues and international affairs. We need intentional work communities such as factories. We need a seminary for the training of ministers for a new decade so that they go to lead knowing what it is to have been a part of the *koinonia* and what it is to be in a praying-agape relationship with a community, and thus with the world church.

In Washington there are 501 churches, and there ought to be 501 places in the city where the church is serving in a quiet but vital way. There are some people who say to us that they are not interested in our House Congregation and they don't care for the Potter's House and art has never made any appeal and they are not called to be with the sick and the poor, but they are interested in international relations and would like to dig in here. We used to be able to respond by saying, "Well, what we will do is help you get a mission group started because surely it is needed and surely we want the church represented in this area." We cannot say this any more because we are spread too thin and we cannot give the support which is needed to launch a new mission. But suppose when a person came to us and said he was not interested in any of the things we were doing, we could say, "All right, the Baptist Church on P Street has a group which is serving in a way that will excite you. It is vital. It is challenging. You go there and you can grapple with the international problems of our time." Or suppose another church is giving guidance and direction to a drama group and a person says that this is what he is interested in. Then we can say, "There is a church on the corner of 10th and H, and these people are working on drama. They are performing on street corners and in parks and they have a touring company traveling around in a truck which converts into a stage, and some of them are writing religious drama and they have a drama school. If you want to be a part of a committed church in this field, there is where you need to be." There would not be one hundred exciting possibilities; there would be thousands. This is what would shake a city to its foundations. Taking that city for Christ would not be oratory. It would be reality unfolding in our midst, and perhaps this would truly be the "ecumenical century." We would be sending people to the

churches where they could express their Christian commitment and
they would be sending people to us. We would draw from one another and our very lives would be intermingled as we sought to be
a servant church.

For every church, as for every person, there is a new land to go
out into, if it is to know renewal. This is forever the way. We look
at the structure which is the Potter's House and wonder what are
its frontiers. One night last month a minister who had left the
church to take a job in the State Department talked to us ex-
citedly about the coffee house. He said, "This is what I knew the
church should be and I didn't know how to go about it. I want to
attend your church." We invited him to worship with us on a Sunday morning and he came eager and open, but the traditional
church service in our blue chapel disappointed him, and he said in
effect, "I'll stick to the Potter's House." There crossed our minds
the thought that perhaps on Sunday mornings there should be a
worship service at the Potter's House and that out of this congregation might grow a liturgy suitable not only for the market place,
but a liturgy expressing the generation of abstract paintings and
modern technology and space travel—a generation who may need
their own setting to discover the majestic grandeur of cathedrals
and the simple loveliness of blue chapels, the friendship of St.
Francis, of Brother Lawrence, and of Bonhoeffer. Perhaps to the
congregation that would grow up there should be given the task
of finding the new land that the Potter's House must move toward
to know renewal in its life.

A picture of congregations worshiping in factories and coffee
houses and in offices and shops emerges into even sharper relief
when we consider the Workshop.

Four people come to the end of a twelve-week class in weaving,
and three decide that they want to explore another craft while the
fourth wants to continue in weaving. There is the sadness in this
group that we used to have in our little fellowship groups when
they would divide or break up. These four have not lived together
under the Word of God, but spirit has responded to spirit. Perhaps

the unfolding of a creative work was the Word become flesh. Perhaps we just have to give a name to those things of the spirit for the recognition of them to break.

Suppose those who were the committed Christians at the Workshop were to decide to hold their own worship service and to ordain one of their members to the preaching of the Word and the administering of the sacraments. Suppose this congregation were to say to the Workshop classes, "On Sunday mornings there is a small group which gathers here to worship. The sermon this week is 'Christianity and the Arts,' and if this is something you would like to share in, we want you to come." It does not seem unlikely to us that within a short time there would spring up at the Workshop a new Congregation. As its members learned the meaning of worship and prayer, as they began to tithe and to know their belonging to the world-wide fellowship of Christians, they could move out in ways not possible to others, using the medium of art to renew the earth.

We talked briefly to Kay about this and she said with tears to underline her words, "This means I would no longer worship on Sundays in our little chapel."

Some of us looked at Kay and knowing that we were not artists realized that we had no place in the worshiping Congregation of the Workshop. We looked at friends who would be in the factory and knew that we had no certain place there. We began to wonder about the new land in which the Potter's House would find itself in the time ahead. Down what road would the Rockville House Congregation walk? In the next breaking of camp would we be saying farewell to those with whom we had shared our very life? Whatever renewal meant in the deliberations of church bodies and conference committees, did it hold for us the pain of separation? Were these new forms of the church which God had given us a chance to help shape now forcing us out from that which we had known and loved?

In asking these questions we learned why renewal comes slowly to a person, to a group, to a church. We knew also why that which seems to sever us from the past, gives us our belonging to that past, for renewal, wherever it takes us, is always the walk of faith. It is to find oneself in the company of Jesus, of the prophets, and of Abraham.

Go from your country and your kindred and your father's house to the land that I will show you.   Genesis 12:1

Ecclesiastes, or the Preacher, and the Easter Church

I believed the Preacher when he said,

> "All things are full of weariness;
> a man cannot utter it . . ."

He pointed here and there
And everywhere confirmed his words.
My tiredness was without speech.

And then I stumbled on a house,
An ordinary brownstone house on an ordinary street.
But its doors opened on a Life and its rooms were full of music.
I knew that I could run again and not be weary,
And first of all I ran to tell the Preacher.

He weighed me in his glance and made reply:

> "The eye is not satisfied with seeing,
> nor the ear filled with hearing."

I remembered all that I had looked upon,
A hundred seasons that had come and gone,
A thousand learned books that I had read,

Ten hundred million words that I had heard . . .
Each sight and sound betrayer of a promise,
Echoing from empty room to empty room
> down a long maze of corridors.

He was wise, the Preacher, and oh, so right.
But I was drawn to the house as if he were wrong.
When next I saw him, I stood his gaze,
And met him with words that were mine, though someone else
            had used them once:

"Preacher, I say to you,
            Prophets and righteous men have longed to see
                what I have seen,
                and did not see it.
            Longed to hear what I have heard
                and did not hear it."

He was unmoved in his answering,

            "There is nothing new under the sun.
            Is there a thing of which it is said
            'see, this is new!' "

I thought of the face of my friend and it was new
            because I had never looked at him before.
I thought of wind and trees and shifting skies,
            the changing seasons, the cycle of life and death,
            the miracle of growth . . .
And behold! It was all new!

I thought of the moment in which I lived,
Receiving for the first time the broken, sundered past and the
            unknown future.
            And it was new!

I thought of the familiar routine of my day,
The commonplace events, holding now the address of God.
            And they were new!

Across my waking and my sleeping hours
Were the voices of a people singing a new song!

I wanted to ask the Preacher, if he could hear them too,
But he was saying:

            "What was crooked cannot be made
                straight

And what is lacking cannot be
        numbered."

I thought of the countryside that held Dayspring,
        of the blind, and the lame, and the poor, and the deaf,
            who had found a treasure there.

I thought of the Potter's House,
Reminder to a city of a man who watching a potter
        shape a vessel from spoiled clay
Had heard God say,

        "Can I not do with you as this potter has done?
        Like the clay in the potter's hand, so are you in my hand."

I have stopped my running to and fro betwixt the Preacher and
        the brownstone house,
For I understood the Preacher,
        "What has a man from all the toil and strain
            with which he toils beneath the sun?" . . .

Unless eternity can touch it,
Unless he knows the God who makes and loves all things,
Unless his ways be companioned by Him who says,

        "Behold, I make all things new!"

I want to dwell among an Easter people,
I want to know and to be known by them.

APPENDIX I

Courses in the School of Christian Living

Old and New Testaments

The courses in Bible attempt to acquaint the members with the heritage of all Christians, the "rock from whence we were hewn."

The Old Testament class begins with the giving of the Covenant to Moses and the Israelites, then follows them through their development as a nation; traces the revelation of the prophets as they painfully and victoriously discover one attribute of God after another to judge and to comfort, and the revelation becomes the foundation on which we stand; until at last Isaiah sings, "The people who sat in darkness have seen a great light, . . . upon them has the light shined."

The New Testament course teaches of the fulfillment of that prophecy, following the events of the life of Jesus, the giving of the *New* Covenant, the development of the Gospels, the growth of the Twelve, the call of Paul, the growth of the church—watching the weak and fallible people who make up this "glorious company of the apostles and the noble army of martyrs," and seeking to understand something of the amazing power of that first-century church. Such a course invariably ends with the question, "What will *ye*, then, do with Jesus?"

Bibliography

Bright, John D.   *The Kingdom of God*. Nashville: Abingdon Press, 1943.

Brown, Robert McAfee. *The Bible Speaks to You*. Philadelphia: Westminster Press, 1955.

Dodd, C. H.   *The Bible Today*. Cambridge: Cambridge University Press, 1952.

Hunter, A. M.   *Introducing the New Testament*. Philadelphia: Westminster Press, 1957.

Westermann, Claus.   *A Thousand Years and a Day*. Philadelphia:
                            Muhlenberg Press, 1962.

Christian Growth

The disciplines of Christians who have felt the urge to make an
orderly, purposeful response to the love of God have been very
similar through the ages: daily communication with God through
prayer and reading of Scripture, weekly corporate worship, the
consistent giving of money (traditionally beginning with the
tithe), the pursuing of some plan of study or a specific mission engaged in with other members of the fellowship, and a constant
attempt to grow in capacity and skill in the loving of all people
as Christ has loved us.

To the Church of the Saviour come many who have had no
background at all in church life or its teachings. Rather than
intimidation, the disciplined approach is the very thing that at-
tracts those who have so desperately felt the need of the power
of God in their lives. They are only too glad to find a place where
they can dedicate themselves and can embark on a pilgrimage with
others who are also undertaking it seriously and systematically.

The course in Christian Growth is built around an introduction
to the practice of the disciplined life. An early assignment is the
five-minute prayer on arising and a dedication of one's day to God.
As one grows in the art of prayer (a skill gained only by practice), one is surprised to find how quickly the time passes in the
keeping of an hour's vigil in the chapel, or as one stops on the way
home from work to pray in some other church sanctuary.

The bursts of new life and power that come upon the novice
who is eager to explore the Way give the class in Christian Growth
an atmosphere of expectancy. Miracles of healing are not unknown
to the group.

The daily memorizing of "marching orders" which the individual selects from the Gospel according to Luke, for instance,
opens up new interest in the Scriptures as something to live by. At
the end of a week the person who has given it a thorough try has

many exciting developments to report in his attitudes and his relationships with others.

Another assignment might be that of deliberately making acquaintance with two others in the class (one at a time) by inviting them to one's home or meeting them for lunch. Such a plan, followed in the context of the redemptive community, cannot help but set the stage for a new and delightful sort of friendship, built entirely on the participants' common relationship to Christ. All the connections are established within a framework of love; one begins to see the other's good qualities as gifts, and his shortcomings merely as occasions calling forth healing love.

The stewardship of money is learned by practicing proportionate giving for two months. Sometimes elaborate arrangements must be made for this step, a radical one for many. The spiritual effect is that of giving priority to the kingdom in a crucial area of life.

Bibliography

Casteel, John.	*Rediscovering Prayer*. New York: Association Press, 1955.
Day, Albert E.	*An Autobiography of Prayer*. New York: Harper & Brothers, 1952.
Grou, Jean-Nicolas.	*How to Pray*. New York: Harper & Brothers, 1955.
Herman, Emily.	*Creative Prayer*. New York: Harper & Brothers, n.d.
Maclachlan, Lewis.	*Intelligent Prayer*. London: James Clarke & Co., 1946.
Stevenson, J. W.	*God in My Unbelief*. New York: Harper & Row, 1963.
Stewart, George S.	*Lower Levels of Prayer*. Nashville: Abingdon Press, 1940.

Christian Doctrine

A course in the doctrines which are common to all branches of the faith embraces the following topics in nine sessions of guided discussion with a final quiz on the tenth night.

1. Creation and the understanding of the Bible
2. The "Fall"—meaning of sin and evil
3. Beginning the Great Redemption and the meaning of God's revelation of himself
4. A *chosen people* and the meaning of election
5. The need of a mediator or redeemer and understanding of our finiteness
6. Christ—the high point of history ⎫ Ultimate
7. Christ's death and resurrection—the Cross ⎭ revelation
8. The Holy Spirit, grace, and the birth of the church
9. The doctrine of last things (eschatology), heaven and hell, and the meaning of mission

Two aims characterize the course:

1. *A living relationship, not just a theory.* The student is to explore the above-named classical, mainstream doctrines as much as possible in terms of his own relationship to God. No one brand of theology is imposed; rather, one's own deepest spiritual experience is the criterion in questions of the validity of any particular approach for a given individual.

2. *Openness to Truth, or the Holy Spirit, wherever found.* It is hoped that the explorer, whose goal is total commitment to Christ, will become literate in the doctrines essential to all Christian churches, whether or not certain denominational interpretations are personally meaningful to him. He should be at home with Christ in any church, from a simple Friends' meeting to a Roman Catholic Mass. He will have common ground with all Christians everywhere, and if he is thoroughly rooted in it, none of the branches of dogma can threaten his faith. In fact, he will be ever more eager to welcome and explore the Way with other followers.

This is the core of the contribution that the Church of the Saviour would make to the Ecumenical Movement—that of knowing a oneness that persists regardless of even fundamental diversity. He is not confused, because approaches other than his own may be valid and not mutually exclusive. Each, for him, holds the possibility of a new encounter with the Lord of his life.

Bibliography

Brunner, Emil.   *Our Faith*. New York: Charles Scribner's
                        Sons, 1954.

Brunner, Emil.   *The Scandal of Christianity*. Philadelphia:
                        Westminster Press, 1951.

Foreman, Charles.   *A Faith for the Nations*. Philadelphia: West-
                        minster Press, 1957.

Howe, Reuel.   *Man's Need and God's Action*. Greenwich,
                        Conn.: Seabury Press, 1953.

Jenkins, Daniel.   *Believing in God*. Philadelphia: Westminster
                        Press, 1956.

Morrison, Chas. C.   *The Unfinished Reformation*. New York:
                        Harper & Brothers, 1953.

Phillips, J. B.   *Your God Is Too Small*. New York: The
                        Macmillan Company, n.d.

Read, David.   *The Christian Faith*. New York: Charles
                        Scribner's Sons, 1956.

Spurrier, W. A.   *Guide to the Christian Faith*. New York:
                        Charles Scribner's Sons, 1952.

Whale, John.   *Christian Doctrine*. Cambridge: Cambridge
                        University Press, 1952.

Christian Ethics

The course in Christian Ethics aims to give guidance in the application of Christian love (agape) to daily living. It rests upon
the idea that it is impossible to separate the Christian ethic from
the Christian religion. Therefore, the course begins with a look at
the nature of God as revealed in Jesus Christ, and of the nature
of man in relation to the demands of God upon him. Is man capable
of living the good life? Can he meet the standards of the Sermon
on the Mount, which is taken as the definitive pattern for life in
the kingdom of God? The answer is: No—not by himself. If, as
James Stewart says, the gospel is just that we are to take Jesus as
our example, then the Good News is very bad news indeed. For
an ethic of moral example is the most grievous of burdens, bowing

the soul of man to the dust. But ever since Isaiah, men have known that we can have a power that carries us along from within, that gives poise and lift to life and enables us to achieve, at least in some degree, what would otherwise be an impossible ideal. The problem of ethics is at bottom a question of power.

Against this background the course sketches the dilemma of moral man in an immoral society. Conscious of the warfare within himself between good and evil, he faces a situation in personal, group, national and international relations, in which, even when he honestly wishes to do the right thing, so often he cannot. So many of his choices must inevitably be between a lesser and a greater evil. He is faced with the necessity for careful study and reflection as to how, in a sin-infected society, he may do that which is most in line with what he understands to be the will of God. He knows full well that in these matters he must not drift. He can live the "good" life—good at least in intention—only as, through commitment to God, through prayer and worship, he "grows in grace."

Problems of personal growth and of getting along with people are first considered in this course, e.g., truth-telling, the stewardship of time, recreation, group loyalties, courtship, marriage, the search for a creative vocation. Attention is then centered on the Christian attitude toward social problems, toward the state and politics, toward labor and economic issues. Finally, as much time as possible is spent on the question of Christian responsibility and action in war and peace. Sometimes the course is taught by means of a careful analysis and application to specific problems of the principles of the Sermon on the Mount.

Bibliography

Harkness, Georgia.	*Christian Ethics*. Nashville: Abingdon Press, 1957.
Hunter, Archibald.	*A Pattern for Life*. Philadelphia: Westminster Press, 1952.
Jones, E. Stanley.	*The Christ of the Mount*. Nashville: Abingdon Press, 1931.

Kee, Howard C.   *Making Ethical Decisions*. Philadelphia:
                           Westminster Press, 1957.

Miller, Alexander.   *The Renewal of Man*. New York: Double-
                           day & Co., 1955.

Pike, James A.   *Doing the Truth*. New York: Doubleday &
                           Co., 1955.

Scott, E. F.   *The Ethical Teaching of Jesus*. New York:
                           The Macmillan Company, 1951.

Spurrier, William A.   *Guide to the Good Life*. New York: Charles
                           Scribner's Sons, 1955.

Stewardship

Whereas the class in Christian Growth is suited to the beginner who is just becoming aware of the vast realm of new concepts to be mastered and new habits to be formed if he is to embark upon the Way, the person who has lived under a discipline for several years will need, even more than the beginner, a disciplined approach to an ever broadening field. He will find himself involved in more and more responsibility and will receive more and more power as he grows in his commitment to Christ.

This power must not be taken lightly; the consequences of its misuse become more serious as time goes on.

The class in Stewardship evolved to answer the need of committed Christians to find grounding at ever deeper levels. A typical class is limited to fifteen; all are either members of the church or have completed requirements and are in sponsorship. The only exceptions have been theological students who were interning for a year at the church and ministers who come to Washington, D. C., from their pastorates elsewhere especially to attend the School of Christian Living. Thus, it is understood that all in the group are committed to spiritual growth and are already living under a discipline.

From the opening session it is made clear that all in the group will have more than a perfunctory concern for all others. There will be specific concern on the part of each for at least one other person; names are drawn and each is thus given a partner to pray for every day. It is also made plain that much of what goes on in the class may better be kept confidential, in order that the participants may feel completely free to express their deepest insights.

A typical assignment might be the writing of a page on one's philosophy of the use of time and a tabulation of his actual apportionment of it in a typical week. Another might be the filling out of a statement of one's exact financial status and discussion of this with another member of the class. Still another is the relating of an experience in one's life comparable to the breaking of the alabaster box by Mary of Bethany.

An assignment which has brought forth especially gratifying results was the writing of a paper on one's darkest and loneliest moment. The climate created in the class gives the assignments their significance. The accepting atmosphere, the knowledge that all share the common ground of closeness to Christ, and the deep, abiding friendships between class members assure an optimum setting. In it, each one is inspired to give the assignments careful preparation and is eager to read his paper and have it commented upon.

The net result for each student is usually an honest look at his degree of commitment and his grounding in Christ, a receiving of forgiveness by the others in the Body of Christ, and a great surge of inspiration to new and deeper commitment.

Bibliography

Tournier, Paul.   *The Meaning of Persons.* New York: Harper & Brothers, 1957.
Tournier, Paul.   *Guilt and Grace.* New York: Harper & Brothers, 1962.

Spiritual Direction

Basic Principles

1. Spiritual Direction implies the recognition of a certain spiritual authority—at least in a few specific areas. The practice of obedience is to some extent inherent in your relationship with your Spiritual Director, who must be a person in whose sensitivity you have confidence. Your seeking a director indicates a willingness to be guided and to undertake new disciplines. For example, Evelyn Underhill accepted from her Spiritual Director, Baron Von Hügel, the somewhat distasteful suggestion that she lay aside temporarily her studies in mysticism and devote herself to ministering to the poor.

2. It is an open relationship where your fears, feelings of rebellion, critical attitudes, misgivings, etc., are confessed. These matters should always be confined to a Spiritual Director lest they contaminate the fellowship. Your Spiritual Director is one to whom you want to reveal your hidden self.

3. The fact that a person is your best friend does not necessarily mean that he is your best choice of a Spiritual Director. Your Spiritual Director should be able to look at your difficulties with a certain detachment and not be unduly swayed by personal sympathies.

4. Ordinarily spiritual direction is not a mutual relationship, though each person acting as a Spiritual Director should have direction. When the relationship becomes mutual it becomes one of spiritual companionship. While this is good, the element of authority in spiritual direction is lacking.

5. The responsibility of a Spiritual Director is to help another grow in Christ. Special attention is given to a program of study, prayer, service, the disciplines of the church, and to growth in personal and group relations.

6. The Spiritual Director has the responsibility of intercessory prayer, of staying in God's presence on behalf of the person in order that there may be divine light in his directing.

7. The Spiritual Director must be in enough contact to know the currents and movements in the life of the directed. This is a person for whom he is responsible before Christ. Like teachers, spiritual directors will be judged with more strictness. There will be exceptional times when contacts may be as often as once a day, and times when they need to be made only once a month or once every three months.

8. While the Spiritual Director has certain responsibilities, he acts primarily in response to the initiative of the person wishing direction. The Director is not a school master handing out lessons and demanding performance. It is assumed that the person entering into this relationship has already a commitment to growth through prayer, study, and Scripture reading.

Practical Procedure for Choosing a Spiritual Director

1. Pray fifteen minutes a day, asking that God give to you the name of that person or the names of those persons who can act as your Spiritual Director.

2. Having been given the name of a person, ask him or her to pray about assuming this responsibility. The person you choose must want to know and guide your spiritual life as you would have it known and guided.

Period of Directorship

Directorship in its experimental period should be undertaken for a three-month period and then perhaps on a yearly basis. Our recommitment time might also be the time when we consider whether or not we want to continue the relationship for another year. It is always possible, however, to terminate it at any time should there be something fundamentally wrong with it, such as a lack of openness. This should be done only after considerable prayer.

APPENDIX III

General Budget for the Fiscal Year Oct. 1, 1962, to Sept. 30, 1963

I. For Establishing Christ's Kingdom in the World

A. *Ecumenical Belongings:*

Council of Churches, National Capital Area (Speaks for churches of our city.) ————————	$1,200.00	
National Council of Churches (Speaks for the mainstream of Protestant churches in our nation) ———	200.00	
World Council of Churches (Chief spokesman of ecumenical Christianity in the world today) ————	300.00	$1,700.00

B. *Missions in Which We Are Involved:*

The Potter's House. (A coffee house, now self-supporting through volunteer efforts of sixty persons. Has its own budget.) ———		
Renewal Center. (This center of healing is coming into fulfillment at Dayspring this year. It is supported by the contributions of our people.) ———		
Dayspring Retreat Farm. ————————	9,000.00	
Potter's House Workshop. (Our church continues its experiment with art.) ————————	4,000.00	
Rockville House Church. (Our people attempt a community fellowship in a suburban home.) ———	50.00	
Depressed Areas. (This group is exploring the possibilities of setting up a job referral system.) ———	50.00	
The Potter's Association. (Working on the possibility of establishing businesses and industries to serve the depressed areas of our city.) ————————	50.00	13,150.00

C. *Missions Outside Our Fellowship*:

Christian Fellowship, Lynchburg, Virginia. (This
body is primarily college students; it is interracial
and suffers for this in a locale where segregation
pressures are great.) ————————————————— $1,000.00

Wilgespruit Fellowship Farm, South Africa. (An
interracial expression of Christianity in an area
where *apartheid* reigns. This farm is used for
work camps by the World Council of Churches.) —————   300.00

East Harlem Protestant Parish, New York. (Seminary students and others have established
churches to serve this heavily congested area.
The core of this fellowship live in East Harlem.) —————   200.00

Kirkridge, Bangor, Pennsylvania. (Some of our
people are part of this worldwide fellowship of
retreatants who go to Kirkridge regularly for
spiritual enrichment. Our minister leads retreats
there.) ————————————————————————   200.00

Lutheran Inner Mission Society, D.C. (Many of our
people have been helped by the counseling services
provided by this Society.) ————————————————   100.00

Latin American Youth Movement. (An arm of the
National Council of Churches in Latin America.
In the face of social discontent and competing
secular and religious philosophies, it seeks to lead
young people in schools and colleges to Christ.) —————   200.00

Paul Eberhardt for *L'Illustre Protestante,* France.
(The only magazine speaking for ecumenical
Protestantism in France.) ————————————————   100.00

Christian Children's Fund. (This money supports
our orphan girl in Hongkong. She is now sixteen
and looking forward to a nursing career.) ————————   200.00

Faith and Life Community, Texas. (A laboratory
of applied Christianity, complementing the work
of seminary, local church, and campus ministry in
the area of Austin, Texas. Through experiments
in theology and culture it hopes to help men of
faith grow to men of mission.) ————————————   100.00

Seva Vidhyalaya, India. (A missionary training center for women in Madras, India.) ————————————   100.00

Children's Camp Services. (For the use of our own
children and children of our city's depressed areas.) —————   100.00

Ecumenical Student Tuition. (A program held an-
nually at Wesley Seminary by the local Council
of Churches.) ————————————————————   50.00

Urban League, D.C. (This group handles job re-
ferrals for persons in need.) ————————————   50.00   2,700.00

        Total Missions ———————————————————— $17,550.00

II. For Upbuilding the Body of Christ
at 2025 Massachusetts Avenue

A. *Building Fund:* First Trust _____ $ 8,600.00

B. *Church Expenses:*

Education. (Includes Sunday School and School of Christian Living) _____	$ 500.00	
Publications. (Includes Sunday bulletins, Newsletter, Harvest, and brochures) _____	1,500.00	
Conferences, Retreats, Honoraria _____	200.00	
Miscellaneous _____	500.00	2,700.00

C. *House Expenses:*

Heating and Cooling _____	$1,600.00	
Laundry _____	150.00	
Utilities _____	800.00	
Household Supplies _____	600.00	
Household Maintenance _____	1,800.00	
Real Estate Taxes _____	200.00	
Housekeeper _____	3,440.00	
Substitute Housekeeper and Babysitters _____	110.00	8,700.00

D. *Office Expenses:*

Telephone _____	$ 550.00	
Stationery and Supplies _____	500.00	
Postage _____	300.00	1,350.00

E. *Leadership:*

Minister _____	$8,400.00	
Associate (Administration) _____	5,000.00	
Associate (Administration) _____	4,000.00	
Associate (Missions) _____	3,000.00	
Social Security Taxes _____	450.00	
Staff Retirement Program _____	1,000.00	21,850.00

F. *General Miscellaneous:*

Gifts and Flowers _____	$ 450.00	
Books and Library _____	250.00	
Entertainment and Recreation _____	600.00	
Minister's Car Expense _____	1,200.00	
Minister's Discretionary Fund _____	300.00	
Insurance _____	1,200.00	4,000.00

Total All Other _____	$47,200.00
Total General Budget, 1962-63 _____	**$64,750.00**

Format by Mort Perry
Set in Linotype Garamond
Composed, printed and bound by American Book–Stratford Press
HARPER & ROW, PUBLISHERS, INCORPORATED